PSILOCYBIN MUSHROOMS

Psychedelic Mushroom Types and Their Safe Use

Psilocybin Identification Book

Hank Bryant

1st Edition, published in 2020
© 2020 by Monkey Publishing
Monkey Publishing
Lerchenstrasse 111
22767 Hamburg
Germany

Published by *Monkey Publishing*
Edited by *Lily Marlene Booth*
Cover Design by *Diogo Lando*
Graphics on Title & Publisher Page:
Mis-Tery, Irina Skalaban/Shutterstock.com
Cover Image by *Kichigin/Shutterstock*
Printed by *Amazon*

ISBN: 9798561577253

This book contains information on growing psilocybin mushrooms: it has been written and published with the intention of offering information to the public. Psilocybin is an illegal substance throughout much of the world. The publisher does not advocate the practice of illegal activities and advises the reader to conduct their own research in order to gain a thorough understanding of the legal restrictions that may apply to them. Although the author and publisher have made every effort to ensure that the information in this book was correct at press time, the author and publisher do nat assume and hereby disclaim any liability to any party for any loss, damage, or disruption caused by errors or omissions, whether such errors or omissions result from negligence, accident, or any other cause.

MONKEY PUBLISHING

OUR HAND-PICKED
BOOK SELECTION FOR YOU.

LEARN
SOMETHING NEW
EVERYDAY.

Sinuate: Gills smoothly notched before running slightly down the stem

Seceding: Gills attached, but edges breaking away (common in older specimens)

Emarginate: Gills notched before attaching

Free: Gills do not meet the stem (unattached)

Subdecurrent: Gills running only slightly down the stem

Adnate: Gills widely attached to stem

Decurrent: Gills running down the stem

Adnexed: Gills narrowly attached to stem

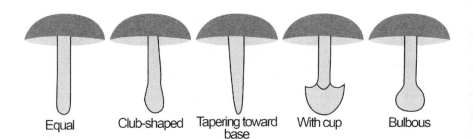

Equal

Club-shaped

Tapering toward base

With cup

Bulbous

DISCLAIMER

Foraging for magic mushrooms must be done with extreme caution. A mix-up with identification could land you in the hospital, or worse. There are many non-psychedelic mushrooms that are deadly. And, as mentioned throughout this guide, there are look-a-like types that resemble the hallucinogenic ones. Be cautious and be smart. Do not consume any mushroom without knowing its identification 100 percent. This guide provides information only; it is not meant to be the sole source of identification. Any mushrooms consumed, hallucinogenic or otherwise, are at your own risk.

TABLE OF CONTENTS

INTRODUCTION

T he world of hallucinogenic mushrooms is vast, with over 200 species occurring around the world. They span a swath of genus, style, type, and effects. Some are rare, or extremely difficult to identify, while others are more common and easily identifiable. This guide highlights a few of the common types around the world.

Each mushroom provides its own particular experience, with no two being exactly alike. The research into these effects is ongoing, with new discoveries being made all the time. Hallucinogenic mushrooms are notoriously hard to study conclusively because the results vary so widely based on type, dosage, and individual. Additionally, where the mushrooms grow makes a difference, even among one type. A species found in Russia may not have the exact same effects as the same species found in South America. In fact, studies of commercially grown species indicate that growths from the same spores are not equal in strength, either. Ecology plays a significant role, as does the fickleness of natural chemistry.

When people think about hallucinogenic mushrooms, they generally only consider the Psilocybin species. However, that is only a portion of the actual hallucinogenic mushrooms that exist. There are psychoactive mushrooms across many species.

Yellowj/Shutterstock.com

In this compilation, the species listed are those that are found in the greatest number of places. There are so many types that have only been found in one location, for example, a lawn or field in one town. Sometimes they are never seen again. Other times, they are common in that one exact location and are never found anywhere else. There are species that pop up in one area, disappear, and then reappear in another city, state, or country. One of the struggles, especially with the Psilocybe genus, is that the majority of the species are extremely nondescript. They are small, brown, and to the average eye, uninteresting. Or, so common that they don't inspire further exploration. Only if you are looking closely, really closely, will you find these specimens.

2

CHAPTER 1

MAGIC MUSHROOMS: A HISTORY

Psilocybin mushrooms grow all over the world, with different species native to different regions. They can be found on all continents except Antarctica, though most species tend to prefer subtropical and tropical regions. These mushrooms have a long history of use in the tribes of Central and South America for religious and spiritual rituals. In modern times, they are one of the most commonly-used recreational hallucinogens in Europe and the United States.

Wakajawaka/Shutterstock.com

One of the most compelling things about psilocybin mushrooms is that the history of their use goes back to the very dawn of humanity. As far back as we look, and in societies all across the globe, we can find signs of their use. There are even some compelling theories about their role in our evolution as a civilized species. While this is conjecture as yet, it's fascinating to explore our historical relationship with this gentle and powerful organism.

EARLY USE OF PSILOCYBIN

Though we don't know when humans first discovered psychoactive mushrooms, archeological findings suggest that they have been known and used by early human tribes at least 9000 years ago. Some of the earliest evidence comes from stone-age art. Depictions of mushrooms can be found in cave paintings discovered near Villa del Homo, Spain and in the Tassili caves in southern Algeria. These have led archeologists to hypothesize that early humans used psychedelic mushrooms in religious rituals.

One theory, posited by Terrence McKenna, is that psychedelic mushrooms were a central influence in human evolution. McKenna has posited that magic mushrooms helped to raise human consciousness to the level of self-reflection and abstract thought. This theory has been criticized by the scientific community as being lacking in evidence. However, current studies into the impact of psychedelics on brain function suggest that they have the capacity to reorganize neural connections and increase communication between different parts of the brain. To me, this suggests that there might be more to McKenna's theory than the scientific community has yet recognized.

To bring this to (relatively) more modern times, numerous stone carvings depicting mushrooms have been found in Central and South America. Many of these statues and murals date back more than 2000 years and have marked similarity to specific Psilocybe species. The Mayan, Aztec, Mazatec, Nahua, Mixtec, and Zapotec tribes of Central America are all known to have used psychedelic mushrooms in their religious rituals. The Aztecs called one Psilocybe species teonanacatl, meaning "flesh of the gods." Mazatec and Aztec names for psilocybin mushrooms can be translated to "wondrous mushrooms," "divinatory mushrooms," and "genius mushrooms."

The use of psilocybin mushrooms was prevalent amongst these tribes when the Spanish conquistadors arrived in the New World. However, the Spanish viewed their use with suspicion, believing that they allowed users to communicate with devils.

Therefore, the use of Psilocybes and other psychedelic substances was suppressed. Efforts to convert the tribes to Catholicism also resulted in the suppression of all religious and spiritual traditions of the tribes. However, tribal religious practices, including those which use entheogens (psychedelic substances), have persisted, often in secret, into the present day.

PSILOCYBIN MUSHROOMS IN WESTERN SOCIETY

Western society has only encountered psychedelics relatively recently. This was largely due to Maria Sabina, a Mexican curandera, or native healer. Maria Sabina held healing rituals known as veladas. During these rituals, participants would ingest psilocybin mushrooms as a spiritual sacrament intended to purify and facilitate sacred communion. Sabina learned about the use of psilocybin mushrooms from her grandfather and great-grandfather, both shamans in the Mazatec tradition.

Valentina Wasson and R. Gordon Wasson were a married couple who were permitted by Maria Sabina to attend the velada in 1955. Their experience was so profound that they sought to make the potential of psilocybin mushrooms known to the West. Wasson collected spores from the mushrooms ingested during the ceremony. He brought these spores to Robert Heim, who, in the following year, identified them as members of the genus Psilocybe. Subsequent fieldwork allowed Heim to identify three species of Psilocybe used in the velada: Psilocybe mexicana, Psilocybe caerulescens, and Psilocybe zapotecorum. In 1957, the same year Albert Hoffman accidentally discovered LSD, Wasson published an article in *Life* Magazine entitled "Seeking the Magic Mushroom." This made Wasson's experience available, at least in printed form, to the West. By 1958, Hoffman had identified psilocybin and psilocin as psychoactive compounds in psilocybin mushrooms. In the process, Hoffman began to synthesize psilocybin, making it possible for the purified compound to be tested in Western psychological trials.

Timothy Leary, after encountering Wasson's article, visited Mexico to gain firsthand experience of the psychedelic effects of psilocybin mushrooms. Leary returned to Harvard in 1960 and partnered with Richard Alpert to begin the Harvard Psilocybin Project. This project was a forum for the study of psychedelic substances, both from a psychological and spiritual standpoint. Though it led to the dismissal of Alpert and Leary from Harvard by 1963, their work and that of other contemporary researchers exploded into the popular field.

As Leary and Alpert continued to promote the psychedelic experience in 1960's counterculture, interest grew. As it did, both the use of psilocybin mushrooms and research into them expanded. By the beginning of the next decade, several Psilocybe species had been identified throughout North America, Asia, and Europe. As these mushrooms are naturally occurring across the world, positive identification was followed by collection. During this period, a number of works were also published detailing how to cultivate Psilocybe cubensis. P. cubensis is a species of psilocybin mushroom which is extremely hardy and relatively easy to grow. This makes it a perfect specimen for cultivation by novices with limited materials.

In the present day, psilocybin mushrooms are among the most widely-used psychedelic substances. They are readily available in nature and easy to cultivate. Furthermore, they have been described in the 2017 Global Drug Survey as the safest recreational drug. Despite this, the active compounds of psilocybin mushrooms, psilocybin, and psilocin were declared in 1968 to be as illegal in their purified form as heroin and crack cocaine. Legality of the mushrooms themselves varies by country and will be discussed in greater detail in later sections.

CHAPTER 2

THINGS YOU MIGHT LIKE TO KNOW ABOUT 'SHROOMS

The Naked Eye/Shutterstock.com

As with anything, it helps to be informed. So, this section provides a bit of background information on psilocybin mushrooms, as well as some facts and figures associated with their use and the use of psychedelics in general.

GENERAL INFORMATION

One of the first things you might like to know about psilocybin mushrooms is that they are neither toxic nor addictive. One common myth about 'shrooms is that they are poisonous and that it is the poison which creates the psychedelic experience. This could be considered to be true–but only if you categorize poisonous substances as compounds that create an "intoxicated" or altered state. In that case, this definition would include every single drug, including caffeine and marijuana, not to mention nicotine and alcohol. However, if your definition of poisonous is something that has a toxic effect on the body, then psilocybin mushrooms do not fall into this category. In fact, they have fewer toxic effects than any of the drugs mentioned above, aside from marijuana, which has no recorded toxic effects whatsoever.

Magic mushrooms do not cause any known major health effects. They do not, as another myth suggests, cause bleeding of the brain or stomach. Nor do they cause kidney failure. A 1981 report found no complication of mushroom use in healthy individuals aside from dilated pupils and overly sensitive reflexes during the period of the trip.

Furthermore, you are not likely to overdose, as the typical "heroic" or massive dose is about 5g of dried mushrooms. To even get close to your limit for overdosing, you'd have to consume about 1.7kg of dried mushrooms. Quickly. And have your body process the whole lot pretty much instantaneously. For the Americans out there, that's about 3 ¾lb of dried mushrooms. Which, if you're curious, comes to about 17kg or 37.5lb of fresh mushrooms. Bottom line–it's not going to happen. (For the math geeks out there, this means that dried mushrooms are 10x more potent than fresh mushrooms by weight. Taken a step further, this means that 90% of the weight of fresh mushrooms comes from water.)

Despite being categorized amongst highly illegal drugs with no known therapeutic use and a high potential for abuse, psilocybin has very little potential for abuse. In fact, it has been shown to be helpful in the treatment of addiction. Furthermore, tolerance develops very quickly with psilocybin and other psychedelic substances, making it extremely difficult to abuse them chronically. And, should this elicit concern, this tolerance also drops within a couple of days after use. A rule of thumb with psychedelics is that, should you choose to trip two days in a row, on the second day, you will have to ingest double the amount of the first day to have the same effect. It makes a lot more sense just to space out your trips.

The same applies to situations where you would like to extend the period of the trip. Often, taking more hallucinogens after you have peaked will produce a longer trip, but will not increase the intensity unless a much larger dose is ingested. Before you follow this rule blindly, remember that each person's body chemistry is different. Plus, with psilocybin mushrooms, it is difficult to estimate the exact dose, so it is preferable to proceed with caution.

Another common fear is that psilocybin mushrooms and other psychedelics will make you go insane. This is simply not the case. However, they do bring on an intensity of emotion and experience. When first exploring hallucinogens, it is of the utmost importance to have an experienced guide who can provide a touchstone during more intense moments. It is also important to begin with small doses until you know how your body–and your mind–will react to the experience.

If you have never tripped before and you are considering the experience, first make sure that you choose to trip with people that you are comfortable with, those that you trust completely and feel safe around. Make sure that the setting is controlled, like a nice quiet, clean place inside where you can lie down if you feel like it, or a peaceful setting outside where you can be yourself and feel close to nature. It might sound like a good idea to trip and go to a club or a party, but if you are inexperienced, these things are almost never quite as fun as you think they'll be. Find out how it will affect you first. You'll thank yourself later.

When first delving into psilocybin or other hallucinogens, one thing that you will want to remember–and maybe have reminded to you–is that you are *not* crazy and that you will *not* be like this for the rest of your life. The trip will come up, and it will come down, and you will feel normal again. In the meantime, just breathe. If you have things coming up, let them come up. Don't resist. Look at what they have to show you and file them away for later. There's no need to make major decisions while you are in that space. That's for later.

There are two major things that you might want to be cautious about when working with psilocybin mushrooms. The first is that you want to know for certain that the mushrooms you ingest are indeed psilocybin mushrooms and not some other look-alike species. This means that you don't want to go out and gather mushrooms based on pictures that you found in a book or online. That includes this book or any other. If you do plan to gather wild mushrooms, it is essential to do so with an **experienced** person who has gathered–and ingested–mushrooms in the area that you are gathering. **Experienced** means not just once or twice, but enough times that you know they're not just rolling the dice.

The second thing is that, while mushrooms and other psychedelics are not toxic, if you take more than you're accustomed to, you may decide to do something stupid, or something that makes perfect sense at the time, but which you would look at under other circumstances and feel that it may not have been a wise idea. Having a trusted guide or sitter can help to make sure that this doesn't happen. Experience is also helpful in this regard, as is choosing your moment. For example, tripping while driving or operating heavy machinery is never a good idea. Neither is darting across lanes of traffic or seeing if you have suddenly developed the ability to fly or do backflips. Perhaps you have, but let yourself come down before you test the notion.

The trip itself will begin from 20 minutes to an hour after you have ingested the mushrooms. From that point, the experience will usually last between four and six hours. It is advisable to take a day prior to the experience to get clear about your intentions and reflect a bit about where you are in life. And, it's equally advisable to give yourself a day afterward to integrate what you have experienced. This also gives you time to get grounded before rushing into work or any other unpleasant necessities.

Finally, you'll often hear horror stories about "bad trips." These are not necessarily a product of the substance itself. They are, rather, instances in which anxiety or other mental disorders are enhanced and allowed to run wild. It's to be noted that you should not use psilocybin if you have a family history of schizophrenia or if you have any known mental health issues. The drug can trigger psychotic episodes. Where you might hear of psilocybin being used for therapeutic purposes for problems such as anxiety or PTSD, this is under strict clinical conditions and with medical supervision. Please do not try it on your own.

If you don't have these problems, just relax and breathe, you'll be fine. In fact, if you cultivate a habit of relaxing deeply into the trip and surrendering to the experiences and thoughts that come your way, you'll likely never have a "bad trip" in your life, regardless of how many times that you have a psychedelic experience.

This is, however, entirely up to you. One of the main ways that psychedelic substances teach us is by amplifying our own thoughts and feelings. If you can accept what's going on within you, you'll be fine. If you try to run from it, distract yourself, numb out, or generally escape yourself in any way, you will find that it just doesn't work. We can never really get away from ourselves. Placing ourselves in these situations–**in safe settings**– can help us learn to sit with ourselves and cultivate a deep sense of self-acceptance.

Safe use will be described in much greater detail in a subsequent section.

FACTS AND STATISTICS

Here are several psilocybin facts and statistics which were drawn from a wide range of studies:

1. In one recent study, 83% of people agreed that their experience of psilocybin mushrooms in the study was one of the five most significant experiences of their lives.

2. In a survey, 94% of those who had taken psilocybin mushrooms stated that the experience was life-altering in a positive way.

3. Psilocybin pilot studies at Johns Hopkins University have suggested that psilocybin therapy may be helpful in overcoming addiction to nicotine.

4. 89% of those tested in yet another study rated high or moderate positive behavioral changes after an experience with psilocybin. These rates were consistent even after more than a year of follow-up study.

5. A 2014 MRI study on the neural impact of psilocybin showed simultaneous activity in areas like the hippocampus and anterior cingulate cortex, areas of the brain for which activity is not coordinated in typical waking consciousness. A similar study found a "dramatic change" in brain organization, where different parts of the brain communicated and synchronized with one another beyond what can be observed in typical brain function.

6. A 2011 study which measured the impact of psilocybin on the Big Five domains of personality (neuroticism, extroversion, openness, agreeableness, and conscientiousness) found that openness increased

significantly after a high-dose session and that this quality "remained significantly higher than baseline more than one year after the session."

7.   Many people report that the experience of psilocybin causes a temporary dissolution of the ego. A 2017 study suggests that this temporary loss of ego could be helpful in constructively re-engineering our worldview. Furthermore, those who have gone through this experience retain flexibility of subjective perspective beyond what is observed in those who have never had a psychedelic experience.

8.   Another study showed that mice given psilocybin mushrooms were less likely to freeze up in fearful situations compared to the control group. As a result of these studies, researchers are considering the potential of psilocybin for the treatment of PTSD.

9.   In a study of drug rehabilitation centers of West and Central Europe, hallucinogens were found to be the least frequently seen drug. They accounted for only 0.3% of treatment requests.

10.   A 2016 study found that 84% of those who had taken psychedelic drugs within their lifetime did so to learn more about themselves, 60% took psychedelics to gain spiritual understanding, and 36% did so to help in dealing with emotional issues.

CHAPTER 3

PHARMACOLOGY AND EFFECTS

O ne of the things you'll want to know about before delving into a psilocybin experience is what it will do to you, both on the chemical and pharmacological level and on the level of internal experience. So, here's a breakdown:

PSILOCYBIN PHARMACOLOGY AND BIOCHEMISTRY

Two of the main psychoactive compounds which have been identified in psilocybin mushrooms are, as mentioned above, psilocybin and psilocin. Considering the biochemistry aspect, psilocybin is indirectly responsible for the psychedelic experience, while psilocin is directly responsible. However, psilocin oxidizes quickly upon contact with the air, while psilocybin is a much more stable molecule. Furthermore, psilocybin is broken down in the body to form bioactive psilocin.

If you have worked with fresh mushrooms, then you will be familiar with the tendency for the stalks to turn a bluish color after they have been picked. This is due to the oxidation of psilocin after the outer layer of the stem has been breached. The more it blues, the higher levels of psilocin and the greater potency. Psilocin also breaks down when the mushroom is dried or heated, making psilocybin the primary active molecule in dried or cooked mushrooms or in mushroom tea, prior to ingestion. The tendency of psilocin to oxidize as mushrooms dry is responsible for the bluish or dark-purplish color that dried mushrooms will pick up around the stems and the edges of the caps.

psilocybin   serotonin

For the chemistry nuts out there, both psilocin and psilocybin are derived from the amino acid tryptophan. In the body, tryptophan is a precursor to serotonin, meaning that you need to have sufficient tryptophan levels for your body to create new serotonin molecules. When you ingest psilocybin, phosphatases in your digestive system cleave the phosphoryl ester bond from psilocybin, replacing it with a hydroxyl group. The resulting compound is psilocin, which is a close chemical mimic of serotonin, a neurotransmitter also known as 5-HT or 5-hydroxytryptamine.

In biological terms, psilocin is known as a serotonin agonist. In plain terms, this means that psilocin triggers our serotonin receptors, producing the same effect as if the brain was flooded with serotonin. Cognitive effects of serotonin have been associated with learning, memory, and mood. Low serotonin levels have been linked to depression and anxiety. Happiness, human contact, and the detection of abundant resources are linked to high serotonin production.

Higher levels of serotonin also stimulate dopamine, the body's natural feel-good hormone. However, drugs that stimulate dopamine directly, like heroin and cocaine, are extremely addictive. Substances that stimulate serotonin tend to have more effective feedback mechanisms which prevent the formation of addictive pathways.

To offer a bit more biochemical understanding, we can compare the effects of psilocybin and other serotonin agonists with those of SSRI's or MDMA. Our neurons all speak to one another by releasing neurotransmitters into the synaptic cleft, or the chemical space between neurons. These neurotransmitters trigger the receiving neurons, causing a minute electric charge to travel the length of the neuron to its delivery point, or the next neuron in the link. Both SSRI's and MDMA interfere with the substances that break serotonin down after it's done its job. This means that more serotonin sticks around in the synaptic cleft and continues to trigger the receiving neuron.

The downside of this is that when the brain chemistry normalizes or finds equilibrium after the active psychological influence of these drugs, it does so by making the receiving neurotransmitter less sensitive. This accounts for the depression or the period of "blah" that is often felt after a powerful MDMA experience. The serotonin is still there. It's still doing its thing, but the neurons have had the volume turned down. With serotonin agonists, however, the receiving neuron is triggered to a higher degree while the agonist (like psilocin) is present, and the brain normalizes by breaking down the agonist. This leaves your neurotransmitters less compromised in the days and weeks that follow.

Another implication of this is that serotonin agonists are not good to mix with SSRI's or MDMA. The immediate result can be intense and sometimes even pleasurable. However, the long-term effects of mixing these substances can be extremely challenging, especially in the realm of maintaining a positive mood and relief from anxiety.

PSYCHEDELIC EFFECTS (INTERNAL EXPERIENCE)

Ok. I'll preface this by saying that there's nothing that I can say that will let someone who has never tripped before know what the trip will feel like. It's like trying to describe the taste of an orange to someone who's never tried one. No matter what you say, it won't come close to the real thing. Furthermore, each trip is different, and the experience is highly dependent upon both the internal state and external environment. However, there are certain aspects and common elements of the experience which can be described, so I'll share them as best I can.

When preparing for my first psychedelic experience, I remember asking some more experienced friends what the peak would be like. One friend told me to pay attention to the moment when "everything was happening at once." In essence, the trip strips away the filters that selectively shut off our awareness of certain aspects of the experience. This means that many things will catch your attention that might have previously gone unnoticed. This could be as simple as the particular texture or color of familiar objects, the sound of words or music, the meanings or usage of words, or even simple situational contexts. There is a range of other influences, which I will divide into sensory, emotional, and mental.

SENSORY PSYCHEDELIC EFFECTS

The sensory effects can range from subtle to profound. Often, there will be a tendency to see colors more brightly and perceive a subtle motion in stationary objects. An individual experiencing psilocybin or other psychedelics may see walls or other surfaces ripple, shimmer, or breathe. There is a tendency to perceive patterns, both with eyes closed and open.

Trails and haloes are common as well. Trails are the perception of an afterimage of moving objects, while haloes are an aura or image which surrounds objects, especially light sources. In extreme instances, viewed objects may tend to melt or form into other images, often continuing to shift into yet another image. Fixed objects in a field, such as the components of facial features, may seem to be further or closer apart than normal and may seem to move around slightly while being viewed.

Often, both visual and auditory acuity will be enhanced. In addition to the visual shifts described above, sounds may seem unusually clear, presented with greater cadence and depth than under normal circumstances. This is one of the qualities which make music such a desirable experience during the trip. This same can be experienced with sounds heard in nature. You may also experience synesthesia, a mixing of the senses where sound can be seen, sight can be felt, etc. The effects are highly personal and subjective, and with experience, you may learn to elicit or diminish these sensory effects through intention and focus.

EMOTIONAL PSYCHEDELIC EFFECTS

One of the principal effects of a trip, emotionally, is for the feelings to be enhanced and amplified. This can be a pleasurable experience or a challenging one, depending on the emotions that come up in any given moment. Memories that have been long suppressed may surface, and with them, emotions that have been experienced long ago present as intensely as when you first experienced them. A sense of euphoria or giddiness might arise, especially if you are in a good place when you entered the trip. Similarly, if you are in an anxious or depressed place, these feelings can be amplified to the level of panic or despair.

This is one of the most potentially therapeutic aspects of a trip, whether it comes from the influence of psilocybin or other psychedelics. At the same time, it can be one of the most challenging aspects of the experience. Put simply, everything we experience comes from within us. It is something that we are carrying around. The trip just makes it louder and impossible to overlook. If we are prepared to feel the feeling, accept it, and move on, then we get the therapeutic benefits. We are given an opportunity to move past trauma in a fraction of the time it might take under normal circumstances. If we fight it, then we are literally put through hell. And the thing is, it's our choice if we understand that we've bought the ticket, and we're taking the ride. Once we've begun, the only way out is through.

Under the most pleasant of circumstances, all you have to do is sit back and enjoy the ride. Make sure beforehand that there's nothing you have to do, that you trust the people that you are with, and that you're in a safe and comfortable place. The feelings can be amazingly intense and pleasurable. You may find yourself laughing at the most insane things or grinning from ear to ear. Or, you might find yourself simply enjoying the subtlest of feelings or thoughts in a quiet and completely fulfilling way.

If challenging feelings come up, and if you have the space for it–and you can see and think straight enough for it in the moment–I'd recommend a bit of journaling. If the trip is still too intense for that, allow yourself some reflective time or lay back and journey. Let it come; let yourself feel whatever it has to show you, and let the decisions about what to do about these feelings come later. During the comedown, you can decide how you would like to approach life based on the emotions you have experienced.

MENTAL PSYCHEDELIC EFFECTS

The mental effects are some of the most profound of the trip, though in other ways than the emotional. As mentioned above, the psychedelic experience can lead to a dissolution of the ego. But what does that really mean?

The ego is our story about who we are. About what we like. How the world works for us. What is possible. What is *not* possible. What we want to do, and what we don't want to do. Basically, our ego is the whole framework of our experience. And this is what the psychedelic experience can dissolve.

Suddenly, you're back to basics. Back to being a center-point of experience surrounded by a field of stimuli. And the meaning that you apply to this field of stimuli is much more flexible than under normal circumstances. It's much easier to be abstract, as the familiar reference points have been stripped away. It's also easier to come up with way-out-there connections, which should probably be re-examined under less altered circumstances. They may provide great insight. Or they may be leading you way out on a limb. Either way, it's best to re-evaluate these insights when you can come from a more grounded space.

It's likely that, during your psilocybin experience, you come to realizations that are impossible to express, beautiful, blinding points of awareness that can change everything–only to have them fade with the trip. It's equally likely for these points of realization to stay with you and change your entire approach to life. Most of the time, for the better. The key is to stay grounded. If you have to write a book for people to read before they can understand your perspective, it's possible that your mental journey has been taken further than it needs to go. That's all up to you, and entirely subjective.

Once again, I'd recommend a bit of journaling. You may strike some absolute gold when in the journey, and you may come upon some things that you simply can't understand from a normal perspective. Sometimes, it will be both at once.

From a biological point of view, the psychedelic experience allows more parts of your brain to communicate with one another. This means, potentially, that you will be able to draw in aspects of cognition and understanding which are difficult to access under normal conditions. It may also mean that the thinking process is a bit scrambled and connections are being made that have little validity. In all likelihood, a little of both is occurring. Save the pieces of gold and see if you can integrate them into your normal waking understanding. If you've never tripped before, you might think this an easy process. If you have, then you know it's as simple as preserving that beautiful insight you got while dreaming. Not impossible, but not possible every time.

One of the most powerful ways that the mental aspect of the trip can be used is to make your ego fluid and recrystallize it in a different form. To do this constructively first requires an appropriate set and setting. These will be discussed further in the text. Second, you will want to listen to the powerful emotions or lessons that come up. These provide guidance. They are the "loose ends" that are suppressed under normal circumstances. Third, figure out how you would like to change your approach to life, people, and experience based upon what has been revealed to you in the journey. This is for the comedown phase. Finally, when integrating these lessons into your life, do so with concrete action. This will make the trip a transformative experience rather than just a powerful memory.

CHAPTER 4

PSILOCYBIN MUSHROOMS AND SAFE USE

Most people who have done a bit of study into the psychedelic experience will have encountered two of the conditions for safe use: set and setting. Set refers to the mindset you hold when entering and navigating the trip. Setting addresses the physical location in which you enter the psychedelic experience. However, there are four other conditions that are of equal importance. These are substance, sitter, session, and situation. Taken together, they form the six S's which help to prime an individual to use the trip constructively.

In this chapter, I'll go through all of these conditions in detail, explaining how you can approach the situation to provide the best possible experience. These conditions are important to consider whether you enter into a psychedelic experience with the aid of psilocybin or any other entheogens. In fact, the substance itself is one of the six S's, so I'll provide the details of this condition with psilocybin mushrooms in mind.

Set

As mentioned above, "set" refers to mindset. When ingesting psilocybin or any other hallucinogen, the thoughts and emotions you carry into the trip will be amplified. Because of this, preparation is extremely important. This holds true whether you are a novice or you have tripped thousands of times. The main difference between an inexperienced individual and an experienced one is that experience will tend to make the preparation phase reflexive. Your mental preparation will have a huge impact on your personal experience during the trip.

One thing that is important to remember is that the preparation phase is equally important for both the voyager and the guide. It is not a small thing to act as a guide or sitter for an individual experiencing a trip, especially if they are tripping for the first time or are relatively inexperienced. If you are the guide, then the voyager is placing a huge amount of trust in you. They are relying upon you to provide an anchor when feelings and thoughts become intense. More than that, they are placing themselves in one of the most psychologically vulnerable states a human being can experience.

During the trip, it is important for the guide to remain watchful while giving the voyager space to have their experience. Pay attention to where they go, to how they are feeling, but do not interfere unless necessary. The voyager is the most important thing during the trip. Make sure there is nothing else you have to do, and that you can be there for them fully during the experience. If they become lost and encounter difficulty, it is your responsibility to call them back to presence with calm and gentleness. Facilitating a trip is an art, and should only be done by those who have extensive tripping experience.

For the voyager, remember that the trip is not a recreational experience. It is a transformative and healing journey, one in which your mind and being are opened to new aspects of experience. The trip offers a powerful opportunity to heal buried trauma, to learn new things, and to reshape the way you approach the world. You can use this time to heal old wounds, let go of unhealthy habits, or tap into deep and profound levels of insight. You can frame the experience to help you work through any challenges you may be facing in life. However, in order to do this, you must face the trip as a sacred experience rather than as a simple drug trip.

With this in mind, try to schedule enough time to truly honor the experience. One of the best approaches is to give yourself three days. The first day is for preparation and clarification. The second is for the psilocybin experience. The third is for grounding and the integration of what you have learned and the experiences you have had. You may also wish to use the third day to record any insights you have received or discoveries you have made.

During the first day, try to remain calm and unhurried. It's best if you can wrap up any loose ends before this day, but if there is anything which needs to be addressed, take care of it so there's nothing weighing on your mind. It's best if you are able to spend some of the day in nature. Try to set aside a bit of time for self-reflection.

If you are inexperienced, it is especially helpful to do a bit of focused journaling on the first day. Ask yourself a few questions:

28

Do you have any preconceptions regarding the psilocybin experience? Do you have any expectations from the trip? Is there anything you hope to learn from the trip? To experience? To understand? To resolve? Do you have any particular goals? Psychological? Social? Spiritual?

As your guide should be experienced with psychedelics, they will be able to address any concerns you might have and help you approach the trip from a calm and collected place. Your guide should also be able to answer any questions you have regarding the experience, to the extent that questions can be answered. Remember that the trip is a personal experience, and there is no way to know where you will take it–or it will take you–before you begin.

A final note regarding set: while it is helpful to clarify your expectations and intentions, it is equally important to surrender them prior to the trip. Trips don't follow our expectations. Whatever you have to address will come up during your experience. It may be what you intend, or it may be what really needs attention regardless of your intentions. Furthermore, if you have done a great deal of study prior to the trip, you may have high expectations of what the experience will bring you. Remember that what we get hardly ever looks the way we expect it to. Just allow it to be, and it will bring you where you need to go.

SETTING

Setting relates to your external environment and surroundings. During a psilocybin experience, you will be far more sensitive to sights, sounds, emotions, and thoughts than you might normally be. It is important to set the space for your session and choose the environment wisely. As mentioned above, it is unwise for an inexperienced person to go into an uncontrolled setting during their first trip. That means that clubs and parties aren't great settings for your first psychedelic experience. You'll want to choose a place where you can be you, no matter what comes up, and where you can behave however you wish without being judged or needing to maintain an image.

If you choose to trip indoors, then you will want the room to be uncluttered and comfortable. You will also want a bed or couch available so that you can lie down if the mood strikes you. Make sure that you have soft pillows and blankets. You'll also want access to a toilet and plenty of water. Another good tip is to have a stereo or other sound system ready to go with smooth, mellow music. Basically, you want to prepare the space so that everything you might want is easily accessible. The space should be arranged so that it brings you a sense of peace.

The second option is to trip in an outdoor setting. If you choose to go this route, you'll want a familiar place where you are comfortable and where you can do what you want without observation or censorship. The outdoor experience is more extroverted and will likely bring a strong sense of connection with nature. Even when tripping outdoors, though, you will want to make sure you can lie down comfortably. It's also an excellent idea to bring along a blanket and music.

You may wish to alternate between outside and inside. If this is the case, then it's best to find an easily accessible outdoor space. You won't want to be driving from one place to the next. The psychedelic experience is often more intense when internalized, when in an indoor space. Conversely, while outside, the senses are pulled outward into nature. You may wish to begin inside and go outside to explore nature when things get intense, or start outside and let things build slowly before taking things indoors and allowing the trip to rise to a strong peak. While in the experience, you will often feel powerful and unexpected impulses. It's best to listen to them, so long as you can do so safely.

The sensory enhancement of the psilocybin experience makes music extremely enjoyable and powerful. In fact, most tribal cultures that employ entheogens in their spiritual ceremonies also include music as an essential element of the process. Music serves as a sensory guide to lead the consciousness from one level of awareness to another. It also provides a stream of sensory stimuli, which can focus and direct the consciousness. In the psychedelic experience, music is extremely effective in eliciting emotions and guiding awareness down certain channels. It can provide the voyager with a feeling of safety and a sense of nonverbal support during their experience.

One thing that you may want to keep in mind is that your tastes may change under the influence of psilocybin and other psychedelics. If you normally enjoy loud, wild music, you may find that this music is grating and uncomfortable. Music with words may be distracting, especially once the experience peaks. You may wish to opt for soft, instrumental pieces that provide a smooth feeling. Tribal rhythms, chanting, and drumming may also be extremely pleasurable. You will actually feel the music as it carries you through the melody. The feeling of the music will intensify when you close your eyes, use an eyeshade, or listen to it in the dark.

You may also wish to make sure that you have access to drawing or writing materials. When the trip is extremely intense, these may lay by the wayside, but in the come up and come down, they can be beautiful allies. The same goes for musical instruments if you play them regularly. You may not want them at all, but it's nice to have them at hand if the feeling strikes.

The main thing is that you want to set things up so that you don't have to go anywhere or do anything complex. I've even found times where blankets were ridiculously complex in the thick of the trip, believe it or not. So, the simpler, the better.

SUBSTANCE

The third "S" is related to substance, but really, a better word for it is dosage. Regardless of the psychedelic substance you take, the dosage has a powerful influence on the experience. One of the challenges with psilocybin mushrooms is that the level of psilocybin varies from one strain to the next and from one mushroom to the next within a single strain, depending on growing conditions and age. There is less variation in cultivated mushrooms than in those grown in the wild.

There is a relationship between potency, dosage and the level of intensity that you will experience. A simple table looks at this relationship just for P.cubensis, which has an average potency of 0.63% of psilocybin.

Intensity	Avg. Wt. (dried)	Avg. Wt. (fresh)
Threshold	0.25g	2.5g
Light	0.25-1g	2.5-10g

Medium	1-2.5g	10-25g
Strong	2.5-5g	25-50g
"Heroic"	Above 5g	Above 50g

The relationship between dosage and intensity of experience - P.cubensis

As you can see, the percentage of active ingredients in dried mushrooms is about 10 times as high as in fresh mushrooms.

The threshold amount for psychedelics is the minimum amount needed to feel an alteration in consciousness. For dried Psilocybe cubensis, the threshold amount for the average person is 0.25g. A voyager will typically experience a light trip after ingesting between 0.25g and 1g. Medium trips often result from the ingestion of between 1g and 2.5g. A strong dose for the average person is considered between 2.5g and 5g. Anything over 5g is considered a "heroic" dose, meaning that this dose can be expected to provide an extremely powerful alteration in consciousness.

For fresh mushrooms you can consider the threshold amount of fresh Psilocybe cubensis mushrooms to be 2.5g. A light dose is between 2.5g and 10g. A medium dose is between 10g and 25g. A strong dose is between 25g and 50g. A "heroic" dose of fresh mushrooms is considered to be anything over 50g.

However, if you are using anything other than cubes, the following information on potency will be helpful.

SPECIES	% PSILOCYBIN	% PSILOCIN	% BAEOCYSTIN
P. azurescens	1.78	.38	.35
P. bohemica	1.34	.11	.02

P. semilanceata	.98	.02	.36
P. baeocystis	.85	.59	.10
P. cyanescens	.85	.36	.03
P. tampanensis	.68	.32	n/a
P. cubensis	.63	.60	.025
P. weilii	.61	.27	.05
P. hoogshagenii	.60	.10	n/a
P. stuntzii	.36	.12	.02
P. cyanofibrillosa	.21	.04	n/a
P. liniformans	.16	n/d	.005

The psilometric scale of comparative potency of selected Psilocybe mushrooms[1]

There is a significant difference in the potency of different species, ranging from 1.78% for *P. azurescens* to 0.16 for *P liniformans*. *P. cubensis* is in the mid-range at 0.63%. There have also been some findings that *Cyanescens* is in fact much more potent than indicated in this table and can go as high as 1.96%, making it even more potent than *P. azurescens*. So please be careful if you use it.

Working from this potency list, we can start to work out what the dosage should be. A rule of thumb is to start with less rather than more, especially if it is the first time you are using a species. Your metabolism is different to other people and you will need to work out how you react and what your dose tolerance is. Remember too that your body adjusts to mushrooms and they become less effective if you take them at short intervals, even if you try to take more to counteract this. So, it is better to find the

---

[1] https://erowid.org/plants/mushrooms/mushrooms_info4.shtml (accessed Jan 23, 2019)

34

right dosage for one time and then wait for about a month before using them again.

Here are some recommended dosages for different species.

#	Species	Common names	Dosage
1	P. azurescens	Blue Angels Blue Runners Indigo Psilocybe" Flying Saucer Mushroom Astoriensis	Most potent of the P's with psilocybin levels of 1,78%. Avoid eating more than an eighth of one mushroom at first. Nearly three times as potent as cubensis
2	P. bohemica	Now usually known as P. serbica. Previously also called P. arcana and P. moravica.	Considered to be similar to P. cyanescens, and dosage also probably similar.
3	P. semilanceata	Liberty Cap Witches Hat	20-40 fresh specimens or 1-2g dried. First timers should limit their first try to 25 fresh specimens maximum. As a guide, if you have bulk amounts: there are 30-40 doses in 500g fresh or 30g dried.
4	P. baeocystis	Baeos Knobby Tops Blue Bells	Strong dose is 1-3 fresh or 1g dry. Potency is reduced by half with drying

#	Species	Common names	Dosage
5	P. cyanescens	Cyans Blue Halos Wavy-Capped Psilocybe Blue meanies	1 large or 2-3 small specimens. Half a gram, dried (Some sources say that Psilocybin content varies from 0.66% - 1.96%, and believe that it is the most potent of the genus).
6	P. tampanensis*	This species develops sclerotia – truffles.	From truffles: 4–5g for a light trip. 5 9g for a medium trip. 10–15 g for a strong trip.
7	P. cubensis	Golden Tops Cubies San Isidro Hongos Kentesh Also known as cubes or shrooms	An ounce of fresh flesh. This can be 2 or 40 mushrooms, depending on size. Average recreational dose is 1g dried or 5g for heroic intensity.
9	P. hoogshagenii		1g dried
10	P. stuntzii	Blue Ringers Stuntz's Blue Legs Stuntz's Psilocybe	8g fresh or 20-30 specimens. 1-3g dried.
11	P. cyanofibrillosa	Rhododendron Psilocybe Blue-Haire Psilocybe	2-5 small or 1 large fresh specimens. Consuming dried not recommended as this species loses 70% potency during dehydration.
12	P. liniformans		Similar to cyanofibrillosa.
13	P.mexicana*	Flesh of the gods	5g for a light trip, 10g for a medium, 15 g for a

#	Species	Common names	Dosage
			strong trip This is a truffle (sclerotia).
14	P. atlantis*	Rare. Close relative to P. Mexicana Fruits of delight	4–5g for a light trip. 15 g for a strong trip. This is a truffle (sclerotia).
15	P. pelliculosa		This is a relatively weak mushroom. 20-50g fresh or 2-5g dried.
16	P. sylvatica		20-40g fresh or 2-4g dried.
17	P. antioquiensis		15-20 fresh or 1-2g dried.
18	P. samuiensis	Mainly from Thailand	15–20 fresh.

*Can also be consumed in truffle form.

Recommended dosages for psilocybin species

To be noted is that some of these species develop the normal mushroom fruiting bodies above ground, and also so-called sclerotia (commonly known as "magic truffles") below ground. They have the same active compounds, but it is not certain whether they produce exactly the same experience.

This table has been organized from strongest potency to lowest. The first two have extremely high potency and should be handled with caution. Numbers 3 to 5, potency is high–handle with respect!

If we go back to the P. cubensis table, the levels of intensity have been given for each dose. You might want to keep a similar table to record the dosages for other species that you try.

At threshold doses, a voyager can expect colors to seem somewhat brighter and mood to be elevated. Music will seem "wider," and the voyager may experience some short-term memory anomalies. The threshold experience leaves the journeyer feeling slightly stoned during the course of the trip.

At light doses, the voyager can expect a significant brightening of colors as well as visual effects like trails, halos, and perceived movement of stationary objects. When the eyes are closed, the voyager may experience dimensional patterns. Creativity is vastly increased and memory alterations become more profound. The voyager may also experience confused or distractive thought patterns and reminiscent thoughts may begin to arise.

Medium dosages will result in obvious visuals. Things will tend to look curved and warped. The voyager will see kaleidoscopic patterns on viewed objects such as walls and faces. At this dosage, the voyager will experience mild hallucinations such as "mother of pearl" surfaces and flowing rivers within wood grains. Low levels of synesthesia will begin to occur. Sights and sounds can be felt, etc. When the eyes are closed, the visuals will tend to take on a three-dimensional quality. At a medium dose, the voyager's sense of time will stretch and distort, giving them a sense that the moment is lasting forever.

At high doses, things start to get interesting. The hallucinations become very strong and the voyager may see objects melting or morphing into other objects. It is at this point that the ego begins to dissolve or split. With a splitting of the ego, the voyager may experience internal conversations, or they may be externalized as perceived elements of experience begin talking to them. They may also begin to feel contradictory things at the same time. At this point, both time and reality tend to lose meaning.

Synesthesia becomes pronounced, and the voyager may experience both ESP-type experiences and out-of-body phenomena. However, by this point, it is almost impossible to describe the personal experience, as it moves into a point beyond words. The trip, when experienced, may feel completely dissimilar to what is described, because it is moving beyond what is impossible to describe.

At heroic doses, sensory experiences become so profoundly altered that they bear little similarity to normal reality. The ego is entirely dissolved, and the voyager may tend to merge with other objects, space, and the universe itself. The experience itself cannot be described. Perceptual and thought patterns are altered so profoundly that they pick up on things beyond anything that can be put into words or sensible concepts.

For experienced trippers, the heroic dose can be used to engage with reality in truly transcendent ways. This dose is not recommended for those with little experience, as it may simply be too intense. Go this far and you are entering freak-out level. It can still be therapeutic, as the complete dissolution of the ego can allow a constructive shift in approach to life and others. This being said, most often a high dose will be sufficient for most journeying intents, and medium doses will work for emotional therapy. However, it can be extremely transformative for an individual to experience a heroic dose at least once in their tripping experience. A trip this intense is like a complete death of the ego, and after you experience that, there's little left to fear.

39

SITTER

The sitter or guide is extremely important for first-time users. In some instances, the guide is termed a facilitator. The responsibility of the facilitator is to create a healthy, calm space for the voyager. As mentioned above, this facilitator should have extensive experience with hallucinogens. They need to understand where the voyager will be likely to go during the trip and meet them there when necessary. Furthermore, it is not sufficient for the guide to merely have experience with psilocybin themselves. Guides for first-time users should be experienced in guiding others through the trip.

Some suggest that the guide or facilitator should be sober throughout the experience. This is a valid perspective; however, another alternative is to microdose through the experience. When the guide microdoses, they are able to stay in the same mental vibration as the voyager. However, the guide must be fully aware of how they will respond to psilocybin so that they can make sure that they will be in the appropriate place for the voyager.

During the trip, the guide acts as an anchor for the voyager. They will take care of all the little details that come up, such as the need for water, food, music, and, if necessary, transportation. (If the guide is responsible for transportation by vehicle, complete sobriety is recommended.)

The voyager is likely to experience moments of disorientation. The guide should act as a stable point during these disoriented times. In some instances, the voyager will become lost in their own thoughts and feelings. The guide should stay sufficiently aware of these mental movements that they know when it is right to leave the voyager to their journey, and when it is right to softly and gently bring them back to the present. This is something that cannot be explained. As mentioned above, it's an art and an extremely important one. Nothing more than extensive experience can prepare an individual to sit vigil for a voyager.

In no circumstance should an inexperienced person sit without a guide. However, this being said, there are some people who are naturally disposed to the psychedelic experience and others who find it more difficult to navigate a trip. If you are an individual who is naturally disposed to the psychedelic experience, then you may not need a guide. The problem is that there is no way to know this until you have tripped several times yourself.

The key is to stay calm, breathe, and relax. Remember that the experience will end in its own time and that you will be completely fine. When things get really challenging, all you have to do is wait it out. And, most of all **Don't Panic!** If you can remember that in the trip, then everything will work out fine. But it can be more difficult to keep these things in mind while tripping than you might expect. So, *please* find someone who can guide you through your experience before choosing to take a psychedelic substance for the first time.

At the very least, if an experienced person is unavailable, find a trusted friend who can watch out for you as you trip. Also, make sure that you carefully attend to set, setting, substance, session, and situation.

SESSION

The fifth S, Session, is associated with the time taken for the journey and the stages involved. Each trip involves a series of six stages. These six stages are: ingesting the psychedelic, the initial onset, opening up and letting go, the plateau, the gentle glide, and the end of the formal session.

Understanding the stages of the trip can be extremely helpful for first-time users, both in knowing what to expect and in being able to navigate the trip as they experience it. Knowing the stages can give a novice an understanding of the hour-by-hour progression of the session. The specific experience will differ from person to person and trip to trip, however, the stages remain the same. Here is a description of each stage:

STAGE 1: INGESTING THE PSYCHEDELIC

With regard to external experience, Stage 1 is pretty self-explanatory. With psilocybin mushrooms, this is the time that you eat the mushrooms or drink the mushroom tea. However, there are a few tips that will help you to navigate the experience from here on in.

The first tip is to check the clock when ingesting the 'shrooms. As soon as the psilocybin begins to kick in, your time sense will begin to become distorted. So, you'll want to have a solid clock-check before things get going. Often, you'll begin to feel the effects within about 20 minutes to a half hour. In some instances, it may take up to one hour. So, don't worry if it takes a little while to kick in. It will happen, so long as you have taken the threshold amount for your personal body chemistry. And when you're inexperienced, it's better to err on the side of caution than to take more because you have become impatient.

The second invaluable tip for this stage is to RELAX. When you ingest the mushroom, or right before you do so, take a breath and let it out all the way. If you meditate, then now's the time to enter the meditative state. Let go of everything, and let this be the state from which you enter the trip. This will pay off more than you may imagine over the next several hours.

If you are a first-time user and still have anxiety about the trip, you may wish to speak to your guide for last-minute reassurances. However, at this point, it's best if you have those out of the way. You've bought the ticket. You're taking the ride. All you can do is just let go and let the trip take you where it wants to take you.

STAGE 2: INITIAL ONSET

As you begin to feel the effects, you may wish to lie down. Or not. If you're outside, the effects can be amazing if you are walking around. There are no set rules. Just let the energy take you where it wants to take you. Essentially, the energy will rise up and your senses will begin to become crisper. Your sense of reality and time may begin to waver as the first effects of psilocybin begin to hit. Once again, breathe, meditate (if you're the type of person that meditates), and make sure that you're near where you want to be when it really hits.

The breath is the key. Breath keeps us in tune with our bodies and with the moment. It is like the steady beat of a drum that can keep us focused and in rhythm. Your breath is your best friend, all the way through the trip. Use it to find a path to relaxation. Remember, relaxing and surrendering will make the trip the best experience it can be.

During this time, you will begin to feel slightly inebriated. You may wish to start the music at this point, if you have chosen to include it in your experience, and if it is available. Observe all five senses. Tune in to what your body is experiencing right now. As the rushes of different impressions, thoughts, and images come in, allow them to wash over you. See them as an observer, watching everything without trying to control anything.

STAGE 3: OPENING AND LETTING GO

The initial build-up will lead to the peak, the point of opening up and letting go. This is the point where the trip peaks and you first begin feeling the full effects. Senses are heightened, time begins to become ever more slippery, and interesting thoughts come in. At this point, it's important to remind yourself to let go of any expectations. What will happen, will happen. Just let it be.

You don't have to make any decisions during the peak. You don't have anything to do other than to experience what the trip brings to you. This stage usually lasts about two to three hours, and it is the time that brings you fully into the consciousness of the trip. Thoughts and emotions are enhanced. Your sight begins to shift and flow. Your thoughts begin to depart from their typical path, and anything that is shown to you is part of this journey, whether pleasant or unpleasant. Try to simply allow whatever comes in.

The more you are able to fully let go of control, the more you allow yourself to move into the heart of the experience. At this time, you may experience unusual thoughts or feelings. Some of them may be old baggage coming up to be seen. Other feelings may simply be unusual and without context, but they are all part of the journey. You may feel yourself an alien or outsider. Or, you may feel like you're actually seeing what's around you for the first time ever. Embrace whatever feeling you experience. If you are having a hard time with it, turn to your guide. They'll help you along the way.

STAGE 4: PLATEAU

After about two to three hours have passed, you've stepped fully into the trip. The new feelings that came in over the last few hours have normalized, and this is your new state of being.

Remember, you will come down. You'll be normal eventually. But, this time is valuable. Thoughts about your life will continue to roll through, and now new insights will accompany them. Reality as you know it may seem inaccessible, and you will feel the trip strongly. However, this is the time that can teach you the most.

You can check in with your guide if you need to, but often, all you'll need is a little time to put things into perspective. As you do, you will continue to make new discoveries about yourself. You will feel into what you have done before and whether it is right for you or wrong for you, and you will get a clear notion of what you should do in your movement forward.

The plateau will last from one to two hours, though it may feel like a lifetime or three. Whatever lessons you receive in this time, respect them. See them for the blessings that they are, pleasant or not. These messages tell you how you truly want to move forward. In the process of receiving these aspects of yourself, do what you like. Listen to music. Journal. Play an instrument. Walk in nature. Do whatever you feel like doing. There's no wrong or right way to experience this phase of the trip. Do whatever you feel is right.

STAGE 5: GENTLE GLIDE

During the plateau stage, you will have become acclimatized to the trip. The next stage is when the comedown begins. You can think of it as a gentle glide back to a more normal frame of mind, a slow return to reality. Rational thought starts to come back into focus and the inebriation begins to fade.

During the comedown period, your insights are still fresh, but you are better able to bring these insights into connection with normal waking consciousness. This is a time when journaling can be extremely helpful. By writing or reviewing your experience, you take steps towards integrating what you have learned into life. This is also helpful because the insights may tend to fade as rational thought reasserts itself. By preserving these thoughts in a journal, you'll have better access to them at later times.

Sometimes, instead of doing personal work and reviewing the experience, you'll just want to enjoy the comedown and soak everything in. This is a beautiful time for walking in nature or curling up with a nice cup of coffee or tea. It can also be beautiful to lay back with a warm blanket and listen to music as you ease into sleepy, quiet energy. If you choose to experience nature in this time, it can leave you with a deep sense of presence and a vibrant aliveness, almost a sense of oneness and wonder with everything you see and feel.

STAGE 6: END OF THE FORMAL SESSION

At this point, you have come down, for the most part, but you are left with new perspectives and a general sense of openness. If the trip has been particularly intense, you may feel intense gratitude to finally be "normal" again, or at least more normal that you were a few short hours before. The trip will often highlight people and connections in your life that you truly value, so during this period, you may feel greater love and acceptance for the people in your life. In general, you may feel a strong sense of the beauty and preciousness of every aspect of life.

As with the comedown period, this is an excellent time to record your thoughts. If the trip has shown you things that you would like to approach differently, then this is an excellent time to make decisions about how you would like to do so. Any aspects of life that have been up for review or simply shown to you might bear a few words or thoughts. The trip involves a profound reorganization of neural patterns, and these patterns will provide new perspectives and realizations that remain with you even as your brain activity returns completely to normal. Right after the experience has ended you are best able to record or verbalize these perspectives and insights.

FINAL NOTES ABOUT SESSION

Though these stages described above give a fair indication of the general course of experience, every single trip is different. Each person's experience is different. There is no way to accurately generalize the situation. Your experience will be absolutely unique, each and every time you enter into a psychedelic journey.

The important thing here is not to be lulled into a false sense of confidence regarding what you will experience. Yes, it can help to understand the stages so that you can navigate them more effectively. But, in the moment, the trip is something so alive and present that all anyone can do is embrace the experience and dance with it.

SITUATION

The final S, Situation, refers to the time after the trip. That means the days, weeks, and months after your experience. No part of life can be cut off and perceived in isolation. Every moment in our lives is connected to every other. This means that what the trip has offered you really begins, in a practical sense, in the period that follows. This is when you can bring this new awareness into your decision-making process on a day-to-day basis.

Many who journey regularly describe this as the "unpacking" process. So much comes through so quickly during the trip that it may take some time to unpack all of the lessons and insights. To facilitate the unpacking process, a period of personal review is advisable. During this personal review, you may wish to ask yourself some questions:

- Have you had any revelations regarding thought processes or perspectives, daily habits or routines?

- Are there people in your life that you would like to connect with more closely, or that you would like to show their value to you through your actions?

- Are there people that should be left behind so that you can continue to grow and thrive?

- Are there any goals you would like to move towards? Endeavors that you would like to dedicate your energy to?

These are just a few guiding questions. You may find that others pop up for you based on what you have experienced. When making any shifts, remember to be gentle with yourself. It can take some time to reprogram your approach to life. Slow and steady makes it solid and sustainable.

The psychedelic experience can be profound, and most will want to discuss it with others. But remember that it is unique and personal. Others who have not tripped may be unable to understand what you share, especially on the feeling level. So, don't be discouraged if it is challenging to express why you are making these shifts. What you have experienced is valid because *you have experienced it.* You don't need any external validation for your insights.

Finally, depending on your experience, you may either feel that you would never like to try psilocybin again, or you may wish to relive the experience. If you do wish to experience it again, it is often best to have some time between trips. This will help each experience to be as profound as possible. It will also give you some time to unpack each journey before you go on the next. As with everything else, this is a profoundly personal choice, with no right or wrong answers. Feel into it.

CHAPTER 5

PSILOCYBIN MUSHROOMS: THERAPEUTIC USE, PERSONAL GROWTH, AND MICRODOSING

A s this book is primarily focused on safe use and cultivation, the subjects of therapeutic use and microdosing will be discussed only briefly. The use of psychedelics for personal growth is discussed only tangentially as well. Each of these subjects is extensive enough to fill a volume of their own. If you'd like to explore the subject deeper, I recommend looking into some of my other books or the works of many other experienced psychonauts.

THERAPEUTIC USE

In the material above, I've offered some details as to how psilocybin and psychedelics, in general, can be used therapeutically. Testing of psilocybin by the medical community is still in its infancy, as laws have only begun to allow limited investigation within the last decade. The medical community is currently exploring its medical uses for a number of conditions. These include depression, addiction, PTSD, cluster headaches and migraines, OCD, and mood and anxiety disorders. Results thus far have been promising in each of these areas.

It's worth mentioning that initial results suggest psilocybin is far more effective in the treatment of depression than anything currently accepted for medical use. Results come more quickly and tend to be longer lasting than other drugs on the market. In addition, unlike these other drugs, patients using psilocybin for treatment of depression do not need to be continuously medicated for the treatment to be effective. In addition, initial research into the use of psilocybin treatment for addiction is more promising by far than any form of treatment thus far discovered.

Psilocybin also has great potential for emotional healing. PTSD and mood and anxiety disorder are just a few of the conditions that have been responsive to psilocybin therapy. Similar studies have shown that psilocybin has been effective at significantly reducing the emotional pain associated with social rejection.

There is no doubt that further studies will show the profound benefits of psilocybin and other psychedelics for treating trauma and all forms of emotional healing. Given the deep impact of emotion on every aspect of our lives, this suggests that psychedelics may be the single most powerful healing tool available to us.

It's noteworthy that a new research division has recently been set up and funded in the Psychiatric Department of the John Hopkins Hospital in the USA, specifically to look at the potential therapeutic effects of psychedelics–and especially psilocybin mushrooms and cannabis.

In the meantime, some relatively recent research undertaken by Dr Griffiths et al from John Hopkins University[2], is interesting and may provide some guidelines about the dosages you choose for yourself. This research helps to explain why, although it is impossible to overdose on mushrooms from a toxicity point of view and they are not addictive, it is necessary to exercise caution because of the intensity of the effects you may experience.

Griffiths et al were looking at possible therapeutic uses for psilocybin, especially for depression and PTSD, in view of its reported long-term positive effects.

They administered varying strengths of psilocybin to 30 volunteers in one study and followed it up with a similar study with 18 volunteers a few years later. They used dosages of 5, 10, 20 and 30mg psilocybin per 70kg body weight of the volunteer, administered either in increasing or decreasing dosages, and at a rate of about once per month. On average this would translate to about 0.8g, 1.6g, 3.2g and 4.8g of dried P cubensis (and matches our description of light, medium, strong and "heroic" doses given earlier).

Some of their findings are useful:

- Doses of 20mg and 30mg produced a mystical experience for 72% of the group (this would be 3.2g and 4.8g in our P. cubensis calculation).

---

[2] Griffiths RR, Richards WA, McCann U, Jesse R., *Psilocybin can occasion mystical-type experiences having substantial and sustained personal meaning and spiritual significance./*https://www.ncbi.nlm.nih.gov/pubmed/16826400 (accessed September 23, 2019)

- One month and even 14 months after these higher dosages, participants rated the experience as having had noteworthy personal and spiritual significance. Up to 65% also reported sustained positive changes in attitude, mood and behavior after 30mg. The 20mg group had similar results, with 60% reporting sustained positive changes.

- Those who had had the ascending doses (i.e. starting low and getting stronger) reported the most positive results. This result was not the same as other research, which suggests that an immediate very strong experience might have long-term positive therapeutic results.

- Those who monitored and recorded the sessions observed that most reactions increased with the increasing dosage[3]. For example, the chance of the participant crying increased with the dosage; arousal, distance from ordinary reality and happiness were highest at the 30mg dosage. However, interestingly, the highest level of peace/harmony was at the 20mg level.

Also, the researchers found that the 30mg dose gave rise to some unpleasant outcomes.

- It was the only level where monitors reported significant paranoid thinking.

- 86% of the participants experienced extreme fearfulness, and an average time of about 11 minutes of strong anxiety. By comparison, at the 20mg level, only 14%

---

3 Ronald F. Griffiths, Matthew W. Johnson, William A. Richards (2011): *Psilocybin occasioned mystical-type experiences: immediate and persisting dose-related effects*/https://www.ncbi.nlm.nih.gov/pmc/articles/PMC3308357/table/T1/ (accessed January 23, 2019)

experienced extreme fearfulness, with only 2 minutes of extreme anxiety. At 10mg, there was no fearfulness and only 1 minute of strong anxiety.

So, it would seem wise to start with low dosages, with 20mg being the most effective and carefully consider your chances of having a bad trip if you try very high dosages.

PERSONAL GROWTH

While therapeutic benefits focus more on the use of psilocybin and other psychedelic compounds for healing, there may be huge benefits for healthy individuals as well. This is an exciting area of study, as it may provide a key for enhancing our capacity for healthy functioning on numerous levels. Therapeutic studies suggest that psilocybin can reduce the impact of negative states like social anxiety, distraction, and lack of motivation. At the same time, positive mental resources like creativity, cognitive function, and productivity have been enhanced through psilocybin use.

On a biological level, psilocybin has been shown to stimulate the growth of new brain cells and facilitate learning. Psilocin, the bioactive metabolite of psilocybin, stimulates the 5-HT2A serotonin receptors in the prefrontal cortex. This has two immediate biological effects. The first is an increased production of Brain Derived Neurotropic Factor (BDNF). Essentially, this stimulates the growth of neurons and neural connections and the activity of these neurons. At the same time, the brain produces more glutamate, a neurotransmitter responsible for learning, memory, and cognition.

With regard to global brain function, psilocybin dampens the activity of the Default Mode Network (DMN). This is a portion of the brain associated with a variety of mental activities including self-reflection, daydreaming, and thoughts of the past or future. When the activity of the DMN is dampened, it is easier for the brain to form new and different neural connections. This means learning new activities and information.

To put this into perspective, consider the act of concentration. Effective concentration requires present moment awareness. Thoughts of the past or future, excessive self-reflection, and daydreaming are dilutions of present moment awareness. They are processes that interfere with present moment awareness. Though these activities have their place, the DMN is often overactive, resulting in excessive self-analysis and counterproductive attention to memories or future possibilities. When the DMN has the volume turned down, the mind becomes more capable of focus and concentration, allowing us to be more productive and to learn new things more quickly and effectively.

Psilocybin also increases global neural function. In typical waking states, many parts of the brain operate more or less independently from one another. Psilocybin causes these parts of the brain to synchronize with one another, allowing more of the brain to operate as a whole rather than a collection of parts. The communication between these various regions is strengthened, and the linkages formed during the trip tend to persist even after the psychedelic experience has ended. In the process, the brain is "rebooted." It is reprogrammed and the neural activity is significantly reorganized.

Despite the advances of medical science, we still know very little about the brain compared to what is left to be discovered.

Because of this, we cannot conclusively determine the impact of this reorganization. However, anecdotal evidence suggests that it is linked to greater empathy and compassion, higher levels of creativity and innovative thought, and the capacity to overcome fear-based blockages. These are just a few of the most profound and oft-cited results that have been described in the bulk of those who have used psilocybin.

As mentioned above, this is a subject that can be discussed extensively, and this book is dedicated more to safe use and psilocybin mushroom cultivation. However, before moving on, it is worthwhile to mention that moderate doses of psilocybin have been shown to shift the brain waves to the alpha rhythm, a state observed in both meditation and flow states. Higher doses have been linked to a dissolution of the ego, which, in turn, provides an opportunity to restructure our perception of ourselves and the world.

MICRODOSING

The use of psilocybin mushrooms and other psychedelics has historically been linked to powerful hallucinogenic experiences. Early research focused on the potential of psychedelics to induce mind-expanding spiritual experiences. These experiences were based on the capacity of large doses of psychedelic compounds to elicit profound changes in the perception of reality. However, in recent years, the practice of microdosing has been gaining attention. This involves the use of psychedelics to gain cognitive benefits without entering a full-blown trip.

Microdosing has, to some extent, increased the legitimacy of psychedelic use. One reason for this is that it is becoming popular among professionals in competitive industries such as those in Silicon Valley. By using a small amount of psilocybin or other psychedelic compounds, professionals are able to gain a competitive edge. Microdosing can help a user to increase creativity and productivity while reducing the effects of anxiety and depression. Furthermore, this is a practice that can have lasting benefits, even after the regimen has been completed.

Essentially, microdosing is exactly what it sounds like. When on a psilocybin mushroom microdosing regimen, a user will ingest a small, measured dose of psilocybin mushrooms. The effect is sub-perceptual, meaning that it is below the amount needed for a psychedelic experience. After ingestion, the user will then go about work or their regular routine just as they would under normal circumstances.

Though the psychological effects are subtle, the benefits can still be profound. They include improved energy levels, problem-solving capacity, and focus. Anecdotal evidence also suggests that microdosing is helpful for breaking unhealthy habits and cultivating healthy ones, increasing connection with nature, improving diet, and improving relationships.

The process of microdosing psilocybin mushrooms is fairly simple. You'll want to begin with a batch of dried mushrooms. Psilocybin content can vary widely from one strain to the next and even from one mushroom to another in the same strain. Because of this, it is helpful to powder the entire batch and mix it together to equalize the levels of psilocybin throughout the batch. If you begin with fresh mushrooms, it will be helpful to boil a measured amount into a tea. Measure the weight of fresh mushrooms that go into the tea, and divide the volume of the resulting tea so that each dosage corresponds to 1g of the starting mass.

For most people, 0.1g of dried mushrooms or 1g of fresh mushrooms will be sufficient to gain the benefits of microdosing. You can use this as a starter dose and then adjust levels as necessary. The goal is to have enough so that you experience very little change in mood, mindset, or disposition, while still feeling extremely subtle effects. You may also need to "recalibrate" with each new batch. This is why it is helpful to have one of the microdosing days on the weekend. It's best to have a bit of a buffer in case the new batch is more potent than the previous. Most of the time, it's not all that fun to be full-on tripping at work.

Another key to microdosing is to set up a schedule. Tolerance will increase quickly, so it is ideal to give yourself two days between each dose. If you want to set up a weekly schedule, for example, you may wish to dose on Wednesday and Sunday. By dosing twice per week, you will gain the full benefits of microdosing without increasing tolerance and needing to up the dosage. Alternately, you can simply dose every three days. For example, dose on day 1, take days 2 and 3 off, then dose again on day 4.

Because microdosing is intended as a means of improving performance and generally enhancing life experience, it will help to keep a journal of the effects. You may wish to note the amount that you have ingested and any specific results you have noticed throughout the course of the day or week. Since psilocybin causes a reorganization of neural activity, it is helpful to record any observations during the off-days as well.

Plus, it is helpful to have records when experimenting with different dosages. You may wish to assess results in areas like productivity, creativity, anxiety, and focus. Different dosages will have different effects on each area, so keeping records will help you to find your "sweet spot" for different activities and effects.

When first beginning your microdosing regimen, you may wish to do so on a day off work. This will help you to become accustomed to the feeling and to make sure the dosage is right for you. You may wish to follow the regimen for several weeks to a few months at first, and then take some time off. In the process, you will be able to observe and record the short-term and long-term effects, and see how these effects persist after the regimen has been completed.

Remember that the goal is to integrate these benefits into your daily life without becoming dependent upon the psychedelic substance. With infrequent use, psilocybin can be leveraged as an occasional advantage. In addition, you'll find that the benefits will remain with you even when you are not actively ingesting psilocybin mushrooms. They essentially lead the way to productive mental and emotional states. This can help you to access these states without assistance in the future.

Finally, despite the numerous benefits of microdosing and of psychedelics in general, it is important to remember that these substances are not magical cure-alls. They can facilitate personal growth and healing, but it requires intention and focus to leverage these effects for lasting benefits. Plus, the key to the benefits provided by psilocybin and other psychedelics is awareness. Essentially, mindfulness. Psilocybin helps us to actively engage with our mental state. By becoming more aware of our internal states, our emotions, our thoughts, and our focus, we constructively harness our attention and access more of our natural potential.

CHAPTER 6

TIPS ON CONSUMPTION

I n the previous chapters, we focused on the experience you may have after ingesting magic mushrooms and on ensuring that you set yourself up for a safe and satisfying journey.

This chapter gives some practical tips about the best ways to actually consume the mushrooms. This may sound a lot more mundane, but it is important to ensure that you have the best experience.

A word of caution: If you are not going to cultivate your own psilocybins, be very careful of your sources. Aside from the danger of being sold a poisonous mushroom, there are imposters waiting to take your cash. According to the *European Monitoring Center for Drugs and Drug Addiction,* in a study of 886 samples sold as hallucinogenic mushrooms in the USA, only 28% were actually so. 35% of the sample proved to be normal edible mushrooms laced with drugs, mainly LSD or PCP (phencyclidine). The rest contained no drug at all.

WAYS TO CONSUME PSILOCYBIN

Not surprisingly, there are many ways for you to ingest psilocybins, some safer than others. We would not recommend that you sniff, smoke or inject them. We also recommend that you <u>never</u> take magic mushrooms together with other drugs, especially alcohol and cannabis.

Rather, we would suggest that you take them orally. You can eat them raw or cooked with other foods to mask their bitter taste. They can be fresh or dried. Dried truffles can generally be substituted for dried mushrooms. You can mix them with something else–peanut butter and honey seem to be popular. Making teas is quick and easy. You can crush dried mushrooms or truffles and sprinkle them over foods or even make your own capsules for microdosing (remember to keep each capsule below 0.5g for this). You can find a list of recipes for your magic mushrooms in the Appendix.

GENERAL TIPS ON CONSUMPTION

Before we continue with recipes, there are a few general tips that you might want to keep in mind.

1. Nausea

Nausea may be the result of the taste or it can be a side effect of the drug. This can be accompanied by severe stomach cramps and even vomiting. To avoid this–and also to get a faster reaction–it's best to take the mushrooms on an empty stomach. Wait for about 2.5 hours after your last meal.

Making a tea and then straining out the solid bits also helps– nausea is caused by the indigestible chitin parts.

Magic mushrooms tend to suppress your appetite, but you might need to eat something during your trip. Fresh, healthy snacks are best–oranges, celery sticks, and non-fatty protein.

2. Water

Magic mushrooms are not toxic, but your body recognizes them as a chemical to be eliminated and will try to flush them from your system. If you are not drinking sufficient water, your body will draw it from other sources and you'll end up being dehydrated. Water will not alter the strength or the duration of the trip. Make sure you have placed about a liter of water near to you before you start–later on, even simple things like fetching a drink can become too complicated.

3. Chewing

Be sure to chew the mushrooms well as this starts the process of releasing the psychoactive compound. Otherwise, invest in a truffle grinder or coffee grinder and grind them to a paste. This may also reduce the time you have to taste them! Another tip is to add the mushrooms to your favorite smoothie. Pulse the blender a few times to mix in well.

4. Heat

Heat kills the active compound. Psilocybin breaks down at 200°C (about 390°F). So, it's better to add mushrooms to foods after they have been cooked–for example on top of an already cooked pizza or into a sauce or a pesto. Or cook for as short a time as possible and on low temperatures. Also, when you are making tea, allow the water to cool slightly after it has boiled before you add it to the mushrooms. When you are brewing the tea, make sure that the water is simmering but not boiling rapidly. However, as long as you are careful about the temperature, you can use pretty much any of your favorite recipes that have mushrooms in them and just substitute psilocybins.

5. Rehydrating dry mushrooms

It usually takes 20 to 30 minutes to rehydrate mushrooms. You want them to triple in size. The warmer the liquid the faster it will be–but not too hot, remember! So maybe use lukewarm liquid and wait for 30–40 minutes. Also, some of the active compounds will seep out into the liquid, so it's a good idea to use any liquid that remains in your recipe too.

6. Lemon and lime

We talk about psilocybin as the psychoactive compound in the mushroom, but it is actually a prodrug, meaning that it has to be converted into another drug–in this case psilocin–to be effective. Usually, this conversion happens through the action of stomach acids. But lemon or lime juice starts the process. When you add the juice to dried or fresh mushrooms, your stomach has less to do and the active compound is absorbed faster, so your trip starts faster and may end faster, but it will be more intense. You are also masking the taste, so the whole experience may be more pleasant.

In general, absorption is better from a liquid, so you can add your mushrooms to any juice. Open the bottle, drink a little, then add the crushed or dried mushrooms, replace the cap and shake well.

7. Chocolate

Chocolate with your mushrooms enhances their effect and can have a strong impact on the intensity of your experience. We recommend this only for experienced users. Be on the lookout for people selling "chocolate truffles"–or make your own.

8. Bad trips

Whether your bad trip is a result of too high a dose or from your own mindset before you started, you may need to lessen the effect. Vitamin C helps–take a high dose of about 1mg. If you don't have any, try a fruit juice. Sugary drinks also help.

9. Potency

Remember to check the potency and the recommended dosages before you just toss mushrooms into your food or drinks. There is some debate about whether mushroom truffles have the same level of potency as the mushroom fruits, but it is probably safest to assume that they are the same.

CHAPTER 7

BIOLOGY AND LIFE CYCLE OF THE MUSHROOM

Mushrooms are some of the most remarkable organisms on the planet, and some of the most poorly understood. Until relatively recently, they were seen as a variety of plant and included in the study of botany. However, in genetic terms, they are more similar to animals than plants. Plus, fungi are geniuses at creating biological compounds. There is so much that they have to offer, and our investigations into mycology are still in their infancy. Between edible mushrooms, medical mycology, and ethnomycology, they provide a rich ground for future study.

The biology and life cycle of the mushroom is a bit technical. However, it's worth soaking up all the information you can about the mushroom, how it grows and what's going on at every level of the process. When you're looking at a beautiful, healthy flush of your own mushrooms, you'll know it's been worth a bit of reading.

About the Mushroom

In taxonomy, mushrooms are classified as fungi. This is a kingdom on its own, distinct from plants (*plantae* kingdom), animals or humans (both in the *animalia* kingdom). It is further broken down into the order Agaricales and the family *Hymenogastraceae.* This is where psilocybe mushrooms fit. They used to be part of the *Strophariaceae* family, but there has been a change to separate hallucinogenic mushrooms from others.

Mushrooms have a deceptively simple lifecycle:

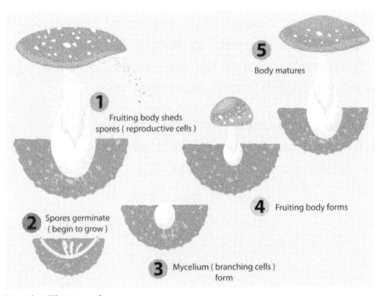

Mapichai/Shutterstock.com

The part that we see, and which we call the mushroom, is only the reproductive part of the organism. It sheds spores, which are the gametes or reproductive cells, that germinate if they fall onto the right surface. For psilocybe that means decaying matter – we call this food source the substrate.

67

They start growing below the surface into tubular threads called hyphae, that spread out into the substrate and divide into forks or fan-like structures. There are enzymes at the tips that break down the matter around them into separate nutrients that are absorbed into the hyphae. The system of hyphae is known collectively as mycelium and has a white, fuzzy, hair-like appearance. It will spread and cover the substrate.

The organism will stay like this until it has "eaten up" all the substrate or there is a change in temperature, moisture, light or carbon dioxide levels. This will make it send out fruiting bodies. This starts as small knotted structures called primordia, also called "pins", that start to push through to the surface of the substrate in a process known as pinning. The cells in the hyphae start to differentiate into all the parts that make up the mushroom - caps, gills, spores, stipes and so on.

Pins are miniature mushrooms – they just need to absorb enough water to swell into full size. This is why mushrooms so often seem to appear overnight after rain.

So far, so good – and this may look a bit like how plants grow. So, what are the more complicated parts? Let's look more closely at the cycle:

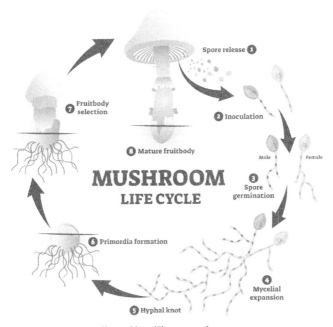

VectorMine/Shutterstock.com

The spores, or gametes, are housed in *gills* on the underside of the mushroom cap. These gills radiate symmetrically from the stalk or *stipe*. Inside the gills are *basidia*, little structures that look like baseball bats, and inside of these are horn-like structures called *sterigma*. There are four spores on each sperigma.

However, each spore or gamete (also called haploid cells) has only half of the genetic material that is required for reproduction. When the conditions are right, each spore will start to grow mycelium as we have described. But this is only "primary" mycelium because it must find a "mate" to supply the other half of the genetic material – much like humans need both sperm and egg. Unlike humans, mushrooms have thousands of genders or mating types, and only certain types will be compatible. (We're telling you this so that when you start your own cultivation, you'll know that from a set of spores you can expect a wide variety of genetic differences.) Even when two mycelia unite, the two haploid nuclei remain distinct. It is only in the gills under the mushroom cap that the haploid nuclei fuse to form a *zygote* or a *diploid cell*. This lasts for just a short period, as the zygote immediately undergoes *meiosis*, and splits into 4 haploid nuclei which migrate into 4 new spores.

As the pins grow, the stipe grows longer, the cap flattens and the membrane that connects the cap to the stalk stretches. This membrane, or *partial veil*, covers and protects the gills. When the gills expand the membrane breaks, leaving a skirt known as the *annulus* on the stem. Water condenses on the sterigma, and droplets then fall and catapult the spores out into the air. And the cycle starts again.

CHAPTER 8

WHY FORAGE FOR HALLUCINOGENICS?

Foraging opens up a whole new world of possibilities. Only a few of these species are commercially cultivated. Many aren't able to be cultivated at this moment. Even those that are cultivated can be difficult to acquire due to laws and legalities in many countries. There are so many species, each one likely providing a slightly different experience. Searching for these in the wild will reveal new species to you, and give a broader experience of the various hallucinogenics. It's also a lot of fun, like a great scavenger hunt!

The low profile, bland coloring, unassuming style, and general lackluster appearance of most of these specimens means they get overlooked by the general public. This can be used to your advantage! Only the experienced eye will see them for what they really are. While others walk on by, dismissing the little brown mushroom (LBM) as uninteresting, you may be striking psychedelic gold.

Unfortunately, because they don't raise interest among the culinary fungi foragers, it means new locations and discoveries get completely missed. It also means that there are likely many more species that have not been discovered yet. Based on what we know about how localized types can be, there are certainly ones that have not been found yet. At least, not by someone who cares what they find. This is exciting and frustrating all at once.

While you may be drawn to this pursuit solely for the potential psychedelic results, the foraging community also implores you to catalog your finds. From a scientific viewpoint, this is just as important.

Foraging is a great outdoor activity with the potential for a real treasure find. Anytime you are outside, look around. Many of these species, especially the Psilocybe type, grow in wood chips or mulch and can be found in cities and landscaped areas. You don't have to go hiking 10 miles in the woods to find them like you must with many solely culinary species.

WHICH MUSHROOMS ARE BEST?

Information on many of these species is still scant, especially in regards to their hallucinogenic effects. Many types have not been studied at all except in their basic identification. The majority of reports on their effects are incidental, a person or people reporting how it affected them and passing that knowledge on to others who are interested. The scientific nature of many of these mushrooms is wholly unexplored. While informal reports are better than nothing, it is not sufficient evidence to give exact particulars regarding the effect a mushroom will have when ingested.

Based on current findings by Paul Stamets, which by no means takes into account every hallucinogenic mushroom, the top eight potent varieties are listed below. Ranking is based on psilocybin concentration and is only for Psilocybe species. It does not include other genus types that contain psilocybin. As mentioned before, psilocybin concentration varies widely between samples and location, making this chart a guide only; concentrations will by no means be the same across all specimens.

Species	Psilocybin %	Psilocin %	Baeocystin %
P.azurescens	1.78%	0.38%	0.35%
P. bohemica*	1.34%	0.11%	0.02%
P.baeocystis	0.85%	0.59%	0.10%
P.cyanescens	0.85%	0.59%	0.10%
P.tampanensis*	0.68%	0.32%	N/a
P.cubensis	0.63%	0.60%	0.02%
P. hoogshagenii	0.60%	0.10%	N/a
P.stuntzii	0.36%	0.12%	0.02%

*rare in the wild, not included in this book

CHAPTER 9

PSILOCYBIN HALLUCINOGENIC
MUSHROOM HABITATS

The fungi kingdom is diverse in regards to appearance, size, and habitat, and this holds true for psychedelic mushrooms as well. They do not all prefer one type of soil or all grow around one type of tree. Each type has it's preferences. Before starting to forage, be sure you understand which habitat the mushroom is likely to be found in.

One common trend that many psilocybin mushrooms share, as far as habitat goes, is that they grow in areas disturbed by humans. Most often, they are found along roadsides, in piles of mulch, on land grazed by livestock, and in city parks and landscapes. Hunting psilocybin mushrooms is counter-intuitive to the majority of other edible mushroom foraging. When people think about hunting mushrooms, they almost always think of the woods, old-growth forests, long hikes, and arduous adventures. That is not the case for psilocybins though.

The best places to look for psilocybin mushrooms is in your home town city park. They grow on dead or dying plant material, which abounds around us. Anyplace that is landscaped is a potential habitat, as well as anyplace that has been cleared for livestock to graze, recently or in the past. Manure-growing psilocybe thrive on the pasture-land humans created all over the world. The more land we clear, the more widespread these mushrooms become.

Psilocybin mushrooms seem to like growing around humans, following us as we disturb and disrupt the earth, letting us know they are here for us. Places where humans have changed the landscape, bulldozed the land and built homes and schools and stores, that is where the psilocybe are found.

LOCATIONS TO GET YOU STARTED

Knowing where to look will make the search for psilocybin a greater success. These five habitats are the best places to start.

Pasture-lands

Psychedelic mushrooms love manure. It is rich in nutrients, minerals, and all the food a little mushroom needs to thrive. Animal dung deposits decompose quickly, in turn making the psilocybe species that prefer them short-lived. To find these types, you'll need to be on the lookout regularly during their preferred season. Often, they will be gone in just a few days, so timing the hunt correctly is essential. Pasture-lands often coincide with grasslands, and if you're lucky, you'll find species from both habitats in the same place.

Pasture-land species to look for: Psilocybe cubensis, Psilocybe coprophila, Panaeolus cyanescens

Grasslands

Meadows, fields, and swampy lowlands are prime psilocybin habitats. Anyplace there is a pocket of grass is a potential habitat. Preferred grass species include sedges, fescues, duneland grasses, bent grasses, and canary grasses.

Grassland species to look for: Psilocybe strictipes, Psilocybe liniformans, Psilocybe semilanceata, Psilocybe mexicana, Psilocybe samuiensis

Gardens, Parks, and Disturbed Land

This is prime psilocybe hunting territory. Rose gardens, flower beds, city parks, roadsides, and along sidewalks are all habitats psilocybin species love. Anywhere there is human activity, like around construction sites, there is possibility. These habitats decline over time, with the most prolific fruiting happening within the first year of disturbance. After several years, the nutrients are used up and the mushrooms will stop appearing, unless there is further disturbance or addition of material, like mulch.

Gardens, in particular, are perfect growing ground for psilocybe species. The natural tending of a garden, like adding compost, mulch, and regular watering, give these mushrooms exactly what they need to thrive. Additionally, adding manure, wood mulch, and various fertilizer emulsions creates the perfect environment.

Garden, park, and disturbed land species to look for: Psilocybe cyanescens, Psilocybe caerulescens, Psilocybe baeocystis, Psilocybe stuntzii, Psilocybe azurescens, Psilocybe subaeruginosa

Woodlands

This broad habitat category actually hosts only a small percentage of psilocybin species. As mentioned previously, psilocybe tend to prefer disturbed areas. Forests and woodland habitats, though, do support several species. A lot depends on altitude, climate, forest type, and water access. Deciduous forests are the best place to look, with the focus on a particular tree type since the mushrooms have generally formed a type of relationship with the tree. The woodland habitats that see psilocybe species flourish usually have streams, rivers, lakes, or ponds in or around them.

Woodland species to look for, along with their preferred tree species: Psilocybe serbica (European beech), Psilocybe caerulipes (American beech), Psilocybe cyanescens (Monterey pine), Psilocybe pelliculosa (Douglas fir), Psilocybe baeocystis (Douglas fir)

Cataclysmic zones, Riparian zones, and Burned areas

Not the most prolific of places, these areas still may host some psilocybe species. Cataclysmic zones, like around landslides and flooded areas, are worth exploring. These places are temporary though, as the environment created by land disturbance isn't the norm for the area. After a few years, the land will revert, or try to revert, back to its' natural state.

Riparian zones are the same. These locations experience intense flooding on a frequent, or infrequent basis, depending on the location. Flooding doesn't just bring on an excess of water, it also causes build-ups of wood, debris, sand, dirt, plants, and trees which the psilocybe use to grow on.

Burned areas aren't great habitats either, but sometimes one gets lucky.

Cataclysmic species to look for: Psilocybe azurescens, Psilocybe strictipes

CHAPTER 10

FORAGING GUIDE

The majority of these mushrooms are small, brown, and rather indistinct. Hunting them takes patience, a good eye, and time – lots of time! There are thousands of little brown mushrooms (LBMs as they are colloquially called), and determining if what you've found is a psychedelic type or otherwise requires a commitment to the hunt. Anyone who thinks they are going to walk out into a field and immediately stumble upon a treasure trove of valuable psilocybe fungi is about to get a rude awakening. Mushroom foraging, in general, takes time and patience. Foraging for these little ones requires even more time and a much greater resource of patience.

Don't get disheartened, though. Just be prepared and know you are embarking on a journey. After all, all good things in life take time. Instant gratification isn't the way to happiness.

There is no one sure way of foraging. Everyone employs their own unique technique, as individual to them as the mushrooms are to the world. A lot depends on which mushroom you are seeking. Hunting for little brown mushrooms in tall grass requires a much different technique than foraging little brown mushrooms in piles of dung.

HERE ARE MY SUGGESTIONS FOR A SUCCESSFUL HUNT:

1. Be patient, above all else. Some hunts you will discover nothing, while others will reward you with more mushrooms than you know what to do with. Take it as it comes, and always be prepared to leave empty handed.

2. Memorize what the mushrooms you are hunting look like. This takes time and practice, but not having to consult a guide every few minutes to determine if it is or is not the one you seek is priceless. Sure, you'll need to consult the guide on occasion, but to easily eliminate the obvious non-matches makes the hunt go much smoother.

3. Pay attention, keep your eyes open, and don't stop looking.

4. Scan, scan, scan. And, when you find that one, don't go running for it. Scan the area, letting your eyes do the searching. Hurrying to the prize may cause you to trample other valuables along the way.

5. Take your time. This is not a race!

6. Know the environment. If the species grows on rotting conifer trees, look for rotting conifer trees. There is no need to spend time looking at every tree.

7. In complete opposition to #6, if several types of psychedelic mushrooms are known to grow in an environment, look everywhere. Overlooking one type because you were entirely focused on another is a common mistake newcomers make. This happens a lot with edible species. A person ultra-focused on finding morels may walk right by porcini, oysters, and other choice edibles simply because they aren't observing their

whole environment. While it's not the end of the world, it is sad that the forager is missing out on so much simply because their eyes and mind are not open to other options.

8. Harvest the entire mushroom, using a small knife to get the base of the stem as well. This is important for identification. Stems are usually where bluing appears first.

9. Harvest more than one, if possible. At least five, if you can. This will help with identification as one may have an indecipherable feature that is clearer on the other specimens. Environment can cause variances between specimens growing right next to each other. Having more than one to use in identification is essential.

10. Note the environment, the trees and the soil where the specimen is found. Take pictures, if possible, of the surrounding area. Take pictures of the mushroom, the gills, the stem, and the cap. All this is important for identification. You may think you'll remember, but if you collect a bunch, it gets difficult to recall the exact details of each spot. Also, if you're out in the woods and it'll be several hours before you can sit down with the specimen, it could completely change by that time. A few hours drying in a bag or wax paper can cause color changes, bruising characteristics, and so forth. Have a notebook with you. Take notes and take pictures. Record the date, the bruising reaction, the flora, fauna, trees, and growth pattern. Was it in a group or by itself? Were there other mushroom species around? Describe the color and the overall appearance. Did it bruise blue immediately or did it happen slowly?

11.   Place harvested specimens in small wax bags or paper bags. Do not put them in plastic, this causes the mushroom to sweat and disintegrate. A wicker basket works nicely as well, if you are careful not to crush small specimens.

12.   When you get your specimens home, do a spore print! See the section below on how to do a spore print. Spore prints are the most accurate way to identify a mushroom and can be the difference between a nice hallucinogenic trip and a trip to the hospital. Do not skip this step.

ITEMS TO BRING ON A MUSHROOM HUNT:

Never go mushroom hunting unprepared. Sure, for hunts around city parks you may not need all these items, but for other adventures, you'll want to be well prepared. People who walk into the woods or unknown areas unprepared sometimes don't come out. It is easy to get disoriented on a mushroom foraging trip. Seeking out little mushrooms on the ground requires attentiveness which could come at the expense of knowing exactly where you are in the woods. Paths linked together start to look the same, and then you aren't sure where the car is anymore. It happens to the best of us. Just be prepared; it'll make the experience less traumatic. Be sure to wear good hiking boots and check the weather before you go out.

- Water

- Snacks – trail mix or energy bars are perfect and lightweight

- Compass

- Collection basket

- Wax paper

- Knife

- Maps

- First-Aid Kit

- Cell Phone (to use for pictures, too)

- Camera, if cell phone is old and without picture taking capability

- Flashlight

- Lighter or matches, for starting a fire

- Money

- Insect repellent

- Sunscreen

- Hat

- Whistle

- Identification guides

CHAPTER 11

HOW TO IDENTIFY HALLUCINOGENIC MUSHROOMS

Besides reading the descriptions and matching the traits of the mushroom against several identification guides, the only really true way to identify a hallucinogenic mushroom is by doing a spore print. Mushrooms produce spores as soon as their gills form and then release them from their undersides. The color of the gills is often not the color of the spore print. Do not make this mistake. Also, if you have any type of color-blindness or visual impairment, let someone else determine the color.

For each mushroom in this guide, the spore print color is listed. Once you've done the spore print, compare it to the mushroom description and make sure it matches. This should be done in conjunction with matching all the other mushroom traits, such as gill type, stem length, and cap color.

Taking a spore print is easy and rather fun. It creates a beautiful imprint of the mushroom in a way few people experience. There is no doubt of Mother Nature's creativity when you see a spore print for the first time.

Six Steps to a Successful Spore Print

1. Select a mushroom that is fresh and mature.

2. Cut the stem away from the cap.

3. Place the cap, gills side down, on a piece of white paper. (Printing paper is excellent for this purpose) [Note: If you think the spore print may be white, use black paper. If you are unsure, straddle the cap over two different color papers.]

4. Place a glass cup or bowl over the cap so it covers it entirely.

5. Wait a few hours.

6. Lift up the glass cup and the mushroom cap, and on the paper should be a spore print of obvious color and shape.

Do not use the appearance of bluing as a significant identifier! While most psilocybin mushrooms do blue when handled, so do many other types. It is important to determine if the species blues, as one step in an identification, but by no means should it be the sole identifier. Also, since most psilocybe species bruise blue, it cannot be used to differentiate between them.

Learn how to key out a mushroom

Yes, this is a bit technical. It does mean learning some scientific terms. But mushroom identification is not something to take lightly, especially if you intend to consume them. This is an important tool mycologists use to determine identification. Remember, the majority of these are little brown mushrooms with minuscule differences to set them apart. And, some have very deadly look-a-likes!

Most mushroom identification books will tell you whether the gills are adnate, detached, free, decurrent, or otherwise. You need to know what these terms mean. The same applies to cap types and stem types.

Please consult the charts (below) to get a basic understanding of mushroom terminology as it applies to identification.

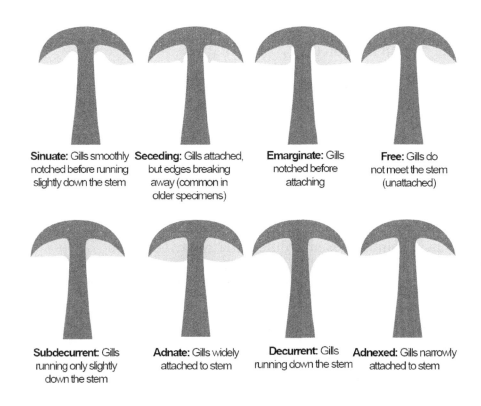

Sinuate: Gills smoothly notched before running slightly down the stem

Seceding: Gills attached, but edges breaking away (common in older specimens)

Emarginate: Gills notched before attaching

Free: Gills do not meet the stem (unattached)

Subdecurrent: Gills running only slightly down the stem

Adnate: Gills widely attached to stem

Decurrent: Gills running down the stem

Adnexed: Gills narrowly attached to stem

Figure 1: Fungi Gill Shapes

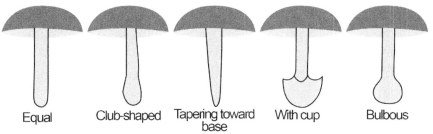

Figure 2: Fungi Stem Shapes

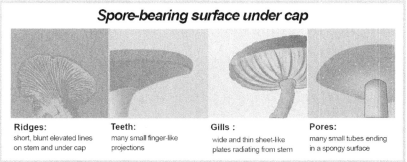

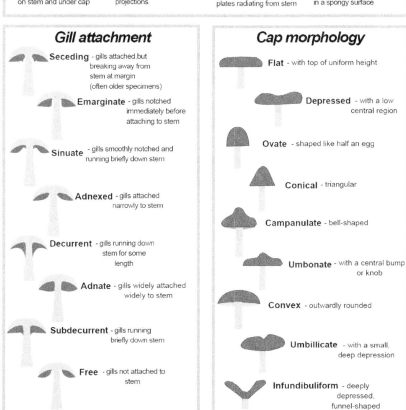

GYMNOPILUS

This genus of gilled mushrooms encompasses 200 different types that grow around the world. Fourteen of them are psychoactive. They all have an especially bitter taste. Some members of the gymnopilus genus quite closely resemble poisonous Galerinas. Forage Gymnopilus with extreme caution and be sure you know the difference between the species.

Gymnopilus aeruginosus (Magic Blue Gym)

Bloodworm/Shroomery.org

Season: May through September

Habitat: Dead wood

Cap: 2-23 cm, convex

Gills: yellow-brown, adnexed to adnate

Stem: 30-120 mm, equal

Spore print: Rusty brown or rusty orange

A gregarious grower, G. aeruginosus is found in clumps on dead wood, logs, and stumps of both hardwood and conifers. The cap is tan or dark brown and often has patches of pink, burgundy, or greenish-blue color. The cap is broad, mostly flat across, and curls inwards at the margins. Cracks often appear on the cap as it ages. Inside flesh of this mushroom is white or off-white. Its gills are yellow-brown to yellow-orange and closely crowded. The stem is thick and roughly the same color as the cap.

This mushroom is a common and widely distributed mushroom in the Pacific Northwest of the United States, as well as some southern states in the US, like Georgia and Tennessee. It also grows in Korea and Japan. It can be found in all seasons except winter. It contains psilocybin and stains green when handled or injured.

Gymnopilus braendlei

Gravija/Shroomery.org

Season: June-September

Habitat: Tree stumps

Cap: 2.5-5 cm, convex

Gills: orange brown, adnate or sinuate

Stem: 2.5-4 cm, equal

Spore print: Orange brown

A fungi with two types of hallucinogen, psilocybin, and psilocin, G. braendlei, is found mostly in the eastern United States and sometimes in the western United States. The cap is purplish-tan when young, then changes to pinkish and yellowish. It will stain slightly green. The gills are white while young and turn to a deep orange-brown or mustard-yellow as the mushroom matures. The stem is tan or off-white. An identifying feature is the green or blue bruising that occurs on the cap and stem. It grows from June-September solitarily or in clumps.

Gymnopilus cyanopalmicola

Season: Unknown

Habitat: Dead palm trees, tropical

Cap: 5-10 cm, convex

Gills: yellowish white, adnate or decurrent

Stem: 40-120 mm, tapered

Spore print: Orange brown

Joust/Shroomery.org

A recent find in Mexico, this tropical species grows on dead palms. The cap is yellow, convex, and ranges from 5-10 cm in diameter. It turns blue when bruised. The gills are yellowish-white, crowded, and decurrent. The yellow stem turns dark red or brown when bruised or dried out. This species is closely related to and resembles G.palmicola, though that type doesn't bruise blue or have psychoactive properties. It grows in overlapping groups or singularly.

Gymnopilus junoius (Laughing Gym, Laughing Jim, Laughing Cap) (previously known as Gymnopilus spectabilis)

MLivezey/Shroomery.org

Season: May through October

Habitat: Decaying stumps, buried wood

Cap: 5-40 cm, convex

Gills: yellow to orange, adnate to sinuate

Stem: 30-250 mm, swollen in middle, tapered

Spore print: Rusty orange

A well-known mushroom, G. junoius is found worldwide, including the United States, Europe, Korea, and Australia. The common name "Laughing Gym" refers to its hallucinogenic properties. However, the actual effects and concentration of psychoactive properties varies greatly, and is disputed by many. Some say it has no hallucinogenic properties at all. In Korea, the common name translates to "bronze clown mushroom." The cap is large, ranging from 7-20 cm across and is yellowish-orange when young, turning to orange-brown or reddish-brown as it matures. It has a thick rusty-brown stem with a rusty-colored ring around it. The gills are attached and are a rusty-brown color. When cooked, this mushroom turns green. Most commonly, it grows in clumps on decaying stumps and logs of both conifers and hardwoods. It sometimes grows singly. The amount of hallucinogen present varies by region and subspecies, with specimens collected in Korea and the eastern United States having the highest concentrations. Some subspecies also contain the neurotoxin gymnopilin.

INOCYBE

A genus with over 1400 species, Inocybe is vast and various. All the mushrooms are mycorrhizal, meaning they form relationships with specific trees. Only a few are known to have psychedelic properties, and this is a relatively recent discovery. So far, seven species have been identified as being hallucinogenic. The majority of Inocybe species contain significant levels of muscarine, a toxin that is deadly in large amounts. Extreme caution is advised when foraging any of this species as they are especially difficult to distinguish from each other. This genus contains some of the most difficult to identify mushrooms in the world. Many have not been tested for psilocybin or muscarine, and it is not unreasonable to think that some contain both.

Inocybe aeruginascens

Season: June through October

Habitat: Sandy areas

Cap: 1-5 cm, cone-shaped to convex

Gills: gray brown, adnate or free

Stem: 22-50 mm, equal or slightly swollen

Spore print: Clay brown

A small bell-shaped brown species, this mushroom is widespread across western North America and central Europe. The cap is 5 cm or less across, and flattens with age, often maintaining a small bump in the center. The gills range from pale to dark brown, and the stem is long, thin, and light gray. A fine powder covers the top of the stem. The stem, gills, and cap stain bluish-green when handled. This mushroom is described as having a soapy odor that is not pleasant.

I.aeruginascens is found in sandy soil around willow, oak, linden, and poplar trees. It contains psilocybin, psilocin, baeocystin, and aeruginascin.

Inocybe corydalina (Greenflush Fibrecap)

Jimmie Veitch/Mushroomoberver.org

Season: August through October

Habitat: Woodlands

Cap: 3.8-5.2 cm, cone-shaped to convex

Gills: pale brown, adnate

Stem: 24-95 mm, equal or swollen base

Spore print: Brown

Named for its distinctive green-ish cap color, I.corydalina is relatively easy to identify. It also has a distinctive and intense odor, similar to matsutake, which is variously described as "sweaty socks" and "spicy cinnamon," or a combination of both.

The cap is 3-5cm diameter, and light or dark brown with a distinguishing greenish tinge. It starts out cone-shaped, becoming flatter with age, though usually retaining a bump in the center. The gills are pale brown or gray, and the stem is cream-colored or tan with a length equal to the cap. It is 4-6 cm thick and slightly swollen at the base.

I.corydalina is found under deciduous and conifer trees across Europe, the UK, and western North America. It grows in open clusters or solitarily in autumn after significant rain. Toxicology reports differ, with some reporting small amounts of psilocybin and other reporting only muscarine toxin and no psilocybin.

Inocybe tricolor

Leif Stridvall/Stridvall.se

96

Season: unknown

Habitat: Norway Spruce

Cap: 1-4 cm, convex to umbonate

Gills: pale brown or tan, adnate

Stem: 2.5-6 cm equal or slightly swollen

Spore print: Brownish red or tan

Found in temperate forests in central Europe, this species is mycorrhizal with Norway Spruce. The cap of this mushroom is dark brown or reddish-brown, bell-shaped, and around 4 cm in diameter. The gills are light brown to yellowish-tan, and the stem is reddish-brown, 3-6 cm long with a slight swelling at the base.

I.tricolor contains psilocybin and psilocin.

PANAEOLUS/COPELANDIA

A broad species of small, black-spored mushrooms, they are most often found growing in dung or in grass. The thirteen types that contain psilocybin are often separated out and referred to under the "Copelandia" genus, as a way of differentiating them within the genus. Mycologists discourage the use of the "Copelandia" title and place all thirteen under "Panaeolus." In written texts, you may see either name used.

These hallucinogenic mushrooms turn blue when their caps and stems are bruised. All members of this genus, not just the hallucinogenic ones, contain some amount of serotonin.

Panaeolus cambodginiensis

Otto/Shroomery.org

Season: Varies

Habitat: Dung, Grasslands

Cap: 1.2-2.5 cm, conic/convex

Gills: descending, sinuate

Stem: 55-95 mm, club-shaped

Spore print: Blackish-brown

A subtropical species, P.cambodginiensis is found across Asia and in Hawaii. It is found most commonly in the dung of the water buffalo. This mushroom is tiny with a small bell-shaped light gray to light brown cap. The stem is long, thin, and slightly swollen at the base, and the gills are dark-gray to black. All parts of this mushroom bruise blue when handled. A potent hallucinogenic, containing both psilocybin and psilocin, this is a commonly grown species.

Panaeolus cyanescens (Blue Meanies, Hawaiians)

Season: Summer through Late Fall

Habitat: Pasture-land, Dung piles

Cap: 1.5-3.5 cm, bell-shaped

Gills: adnexed

Stem: 85-115 cm, club-shaped

Spore print: Black

Alonso/Shroomery.org

This small mushroom is found in tropical and neotropical areas, including parts of Africa, the Caribbean, Asia, Europe, Mexico, South America, and the United States. It has a small, brown, bell-shaped cap with slightly wavy edges. The stem is narrow, tall, light tan, and slightly bulbous at the bottom. The gills on this mushroom are gray or black. The cap and stem will bruise blue when handled.

P.cyanescens grow in large groups of solitary mushrooms. They are usually widely scattered in pastures or anywhere around dung. American states in which this mushroom has been reported include Florida, Texas, Mississippi, Louisiana, Oregon, and Hawaii. The 'blue meanie' mushroom is widely cultivated around the world.

Panaeolus cinctulus (synonym Panaeolus subbalteatus) (Banded Mottlegill, Subbs)

Byrain/Shroomery.org

Season: April through October

Habitat: Gardens, lawns, dung

Cap: 4-5 cm, bell-shaped

Gills: adnate to adnexed

Stem: 50-60 mm, equal or tapered

Spore print: Black

Sometimes called the "weed Panaeolus" because of its propensity to grow in beds of commercial Agaricus (Button) Mushrooms and thus be weeded out. This mushroom is cinnamon-brown in color, with a bell-shaped cap which flattens with age. The gills are fringed and cream-colored when young, then turn dark when mature. The stem is cream-colored or cinnamon-brown, hollow, and covered in white flecks. The stem and cap may bruise blue when handled.

P.cinctulus grows in dense clumps in gardens, lawns, and compost piles. Sometimes, it is found on dung, but this is rare. After a rainfall in the spring or fall, it grows abundantly. This species is known to grow all around the world, including the United States, Canada, Europe, India, South Africa, South America, Mexico, Japan, Russia, and the Philippines. It is extremely common in the western United States, specifically Oregon, Washington, and California.

This hallucinogenic contains mostly psilocybin and very little psilocin.

Panaeolus olivaceus

Joust/Shroomery.org

Season: August through December

Habitat: Grasslands

Cap: 1-3 cm, cone-shaped

Gills: adnate to adnexed

Stem: 4-6 cm, equal or tapered

Spore print: Black

This widely distributed small brown mushroom is easily confused with other mushrooms in the Panaeolus species. The cap is cone-shaped, dark brown with black fringed edges, and smooth. The gills are olive-green when young and turn purplish-black with age. Its stem is brittle, hollow, and gray or dark-brown. P.olivaceus grows in grassy areas in the late summer through early winter in North and South America and in the UK. It grows singularly in scattered groupings.

This mushroom contains psilocybin, though incidental reports state it is weak compared to other mushrooms in the same group.

Panaelous tropicalis

Alan Rockefeller/Wikimedia.org

Season: Varies

Habitat: Tropical, dung dweller

Cap: 1.5-2.5 cm, convex to bell-shaped

Gills: dull gray, adnexed

Stem: 5-12 cm, equal or slightly swollen

Spore print: Dark violet to jet black

Found widely in tropical regions, including the Philippines, Mexico, Hawaii, Florida, Japan, Central Africa, and Cambodia, this hallucinogenic mushroom closely resembles P.cyanescens. The similarities are so close, microscopic characteristics are the only true way to tell them apart. It grows on the dung of wild tropical animals as well as that of domesticated cows.

When young, the cap is smooth, clay-colored, and convex to bell-shaped. The center of the cap is generally yellow-brown towards the center. Its stem is hollow, sometimes swollen at the base, and is on average around 70 mm long. The gills are a dull gray to dark black color. Stem and cap bruise blue when handled.

Pholiotina (Conocybe)

This group of about 50 small, thin mushrooms contains two hallucinogenic types. It also contains a very deadly specimen, P.rugosa. Extreme caution is advised when foraging these mushrooms.

These species previously were assigned to the Conocybe genus. Recent analysis suggests they are more closely aligned with Galerina, and another name change may happen in the future.

Pholiotina cyanopus

maynardjameskeenan/Shroomery.org

Season: July through October

Habitat: Grasslands, lawns, fields

Cap: .7-1.2 cm, convex

Gills: Rusty-brown, adnexed

Stem: 20-40 mm, equal, slightly curved

Spore print: Rusty-brown

This small cinnamon-brown mushroom grows in fields, lawns, and other grassy areas. It is found throughout Asia, Europe, and North America. P.cyanopus has a small smooth cap less than 25 mm across, closely spaced gills, and a long thin light tan stem. Foragers are recommended to be extra careful with this mushroom as it closely resembles several other deadly species (P.rugosa, Cortinarius gentilis, and Galerina marginata).

Pholiotina smithii

Christian/Shroomery.org

Season: April through June

Habitat: Moss, bogs

Cap: .5-1.3 cm, cone-shaped

Gills: gray or brown, adnate or adnexed

Stem: 10-50 mm, equal or slightly swollen

Spore print: Rusty brown

Featuring a cinnamon-brown cone-shaped cap that glistens when wet, P.smithii is a mushroom that grows in small groupings. The gills are light gray to brown with white edges. The stem is cream-colored, swollen at the base, fragile, and slightly twisting. When handled, the stem and cap bruise blue. While considered rare, this fungi is also widespread across the western United States and Canada. It grows in swampy areas and bogs and is commonly found in and around sphagnum moss. This is an early summer mushroom and is unlikely to be found after the beginning of June. The hallucinogenic properties are reported to be mild. It contains psilocybin, psilocin, and baeocystin.

PLUTEUS

A large genus that contains over 300 species, Pluteus mushrooms grow on rotting wood. Their gills are free from the stem, and the spore prints are always pink. Several of the species have hallucinogenic properties and bruise blue when handled.

Pluteus americanus

Dan Molter/Mushroomobserver.org

Season: July through October

Habitat: Decaying hardwood

Cap: 1-6 cm, bell-shaped to convex

Gills: white to pink, free

Stem: 1.5-6.5 cm, equal or slightly swollen

Spore print: Pink or brownish pink

108

This mushroom grows on decaying hardwood trees mainly east of the Rocky Mountains in North America, as well as in eastern Russia. It particularly likes sugar maple, paper birch, aspen, and poplar trees. P. americanus grows in open clusters or solitarily from July through October.

The cap is light brown to gray, and darker in the center. It is slightly bell-shaped when young, it then flattens out and curves upwards with age. The gills start out white then mature to pink. The stem is white or gray, with a slightly swollen base. The cap, gills, and stem stain blue when handled. It is reported to smell and taste like geraniums. P. americanus contains psilocybin and psilocin.

Pluteus cyanopus

Dan Molter/Shroomery.org

Season: August through November

109

Habitat: Old growth forest

Cap: 2.4 cm, flat or convex

Gills: Pinkish brown

Stem: 2-5 cm, equal or slightly swollen

Spore print: Pink brown

This widespread hallucinogenic is found in North America, Europe, and Africa. It contains both psilocybin and psilocin. P.cyanopus grows on decaying hardwoods and possibly conifers in old-growth forests. This mushroom is found from August through to November and grows singularly or in small groupings of two or three.

The cap is smooth, grayish-green, and flat, though it becomes convex with age. Gills are cream-colored when young and turn salmon pink in maturity. The stem is long and thin, white, and has a slightly swollen base. The gills and stem will bruise blue when handled. This mushroom contains psilocybin and psilocin.

Pluteus salicinus

Season: July through November

Habitat: Woodlands, riparians

Cap: 3.7 cm, convex

Gills: cream to pink, free

Stem: 40-100 mm, equal

Spore print: Pinkish

A psychedelic that grows on decaying hardwood in Europe and the United States. It prefers eucalyptus, alder, poplar, birch, beech, willow, and oak trees. The trees are usually in damp forests, and the mushrooms are either solitary or growing in open clusters during the summer through to fall.

The cap is 2-5 cm in diameter, silver-gray or brownish-gray, and smooth. It starts out bell-shaped then becomes flatter with age. The gills start out white then turn pink with maturity. The stem is long and thin, white or gray, and slightly swollen at the base. It is reported to smell and taste somewhat like radishes. The gills and stem bruise blue when handled.

Some reports state this is a culinary mushroom that is edible after being boiled for a while. Others state that since many specimens contain psilocybin, it should not be considered for culinary purposes.

PSILOCYBE

This genus of around 200 fungi encompasses species that contain psilocybin and/or psilocin. Species are found worldwide, and many of them are extremely location-specific. Some types are only found in one city, and even just one lawn or field. Others are widespread across countries and continents.

The mushrooms in this genus are small, cone-shaped, invariably brownish in color, and gilled. They grow on decaying matter and typically stain blue when handled.

Many of the species prefer disturbed landscapes and are rarely found in natural settings. Areas disrupted by human activity are especially common. Psilocybe grow on landscaped lawns, mulch patches, and domesticated animal feces.

The following list describes only the most common, widespread, and notable types.

Psilocybe allenii

Alan Rockefeller/Shroomery.org

Season: September through January

Habitat: Pacific coast, disturbed areas

Cap: 1.5-9 cm, convex to flat

Gills: orange brown, adnate to sinuate

Stem: 4-7 cm, slightly swollen

Spore print: Dark brown, sometimes violet shades

A species found only in western North America, from British Columbia to California, and usually within 10 miles of the Pacific coastline. It grows on rotting wood and is commonly found on wood chips used in landscaping. Identified as a unique species in 2012, this hallucinogenic was known in the areas that it grew for many years prior and was sought out for recreational use.

The caps of this mushroom range from 1.5-9 cm in diameter, and are light to medium brown. When young, they are convex. As they age, they flatten, though they sometimes show a distinguishable bump in the center, or alternately, an indent. When moist, the cap is sticky. Caps are smooth, and the top cuticle layer is easily peeled back. The gills are cream-colored when young and become dark purple with age. The stem is hollow, 4-7 cm long, with a slightly bulbous base. It is white when young and yellows with age. All parts of this mushroom stain blue when handled.

This species grows in scattered groups from late September through January. It seems to prefer hardwood mulches containing oak, alder, Douglas fir, and eucalyptus. It is also easily cultivated.

Psilocybe aztecorum

Alan Rockefeller/Shroomery.org

Season: August - October

Habitat: Woodlands and meadows, between 6,600-13,100 ft elevation

Cap: 1.5-2 cm, convex to bell-shaped

Gills: light or dark purple-gray, adnate to adnexed

Stem: 55-75 mm, equal or swollen

Spore print: Violet black

A widespread species found in India, Mexico, Costa Rica, and parts of the western United States, specifically Arizona and Colorado. It prefers high elevations, ranging from 2,000-4,000 meters (6,600-13,100 feet), and open, grassy meadows or conifer forests.

This species has a convex or bell-shaped cap, 1.5-2 cm in diameter, which flattens with age and becomes indented in the center. The color ranges from yellowish-brown to golden-yellow, with the color change dependent on how hydrated it is. In late maturity, it becomes brownish-gray, and then completely white. The cap is smooth and slimy to the touch. Gills are violet-gray to violet-brown and often have white edges. The stem is hollow, 5.5-7.5 cm long, and whitish-gray. It is sometimes flattened or winding. The base of the stem has visible striations that distinguish it from other species. The cap and stem blue very little when handled.

Growing on decaying wood, leaves, and other organic matter, this mushroom fruits in open groups and sometimes in bundles. It is found August through October. Pine forests, specifically Pinus hartwegii abundant areas, rich with grasses are especially prolific.

Psilocybe azurescens (Azies)

Shroom360/Shroomery.org

Season: September - January

Habitat: Oregon, Coastal Dunes, disturbed areas

Cap: 3-10 cm conic or convex

Gills: brown, sinuate to adnate

Stem: 90-200 mm, slightly swollen

Spore print: Dark purple or black

A species found along the west coast of the United States, including Oregon, Washington, and California, with a concentration around the Columbia River Delta. It grows on wood debris or sandy soils rich with debris in large open clusters. It is also found in dune grasses. P.azurescens is widely cultivated and feral or escaped specimens can be found randomly around the world. This mushroom fruits from late September through early January.

The cap is chestnut to caramel brown, smooth, 30-100 mm diameter, and cone-shaped. As it matures, the cap flattens and changes color, fading to light yellow-brown. When wet, the cap is sticky, and the top cuticle layer can be peeled off. The gills are brown and stain black when injured. The brown stem is 90-200 cm long, hollow, twisted, and thicker closer to the base. The cap turns strongly blue when damaged.

Containing psilocybin, psilocin, and baeocystin, this species is considered one of the more potent of the psychedelic types.

Psilocybe baeocystis (Bottle caps, Blue bells, Olive caps, Knobby tops)

Christian/Shroomery.org

Season: Fall through early winter

Habitat: Wood chips, lawns, gardens

117

Cap: 1.5-5.5 cm, cone-shaped to convex

Gills: Gray to cinnamon-brown, adnate to sinuate

Stem: 50-70 mm, equal

Spore print: purplish brown

This is a western North American species, specifically prevalent in the Pacific Northwest. However, recent reports indicate it grows in New England as well. A species that likes disturbed habitats, this mushroom is found on wood chips, mulch, lawns, pastures, and under rose bushes and rhododendrons.

The cap is cone-shaped, 1.5-5.5 cm in diameter, and stays relatively convex even as it ages. It ranges in color from olive-brown to tan and is even sometimes steel blue. Caps are sometimes rippled. Flesh is thin and bruises easily, turning blue when handled. When wet, the cap is sticky, and the top cuticle layer can be peeled off. The gills are gray to light brown. The stem is 5-7 cm long, brownish with white specks, and brittle.

P. baeocystis grows in scattered groups or solitarily from August through to December. This species contains psilocybin, psilocin, and baeocystin.

Psilocybe caerulescens

Alan Rockefeller/Shroomery.org

Season: June through October

Habitat: Disturbed ground,

Cap: 2-9 cm, bell-shaped to convex

Gills: gray to brown, sinuate to adnate

Stem: 40-120 mm, equal or slightly swollen

Spore print: Dark purple brown

Widespread throughout Brazil, Venezuela, central Mexico, and one US state, Georgia. It was initially found in the United States on sugarcane mulch in Alabama in 1923. It hasn't been seen since in that location, however, it is widespread in northern Georgia. It is also reported in South Carolina. Both the Georgia and

S.Carolina findings were recent (early 2000's) which may mean it is spreading or is already more widespread than documented.

The bell-shaped cap is yellowish to reddish-brown, with an overall bluish-silver luster. When wet, the cap peels easily. Cap shape and color vary greatly with this specimen. When young, the gills are white or yellow-gray, turning brown as they age. The stem is 2-13 cm long, slightly swollen at the base, and hollow. Stems range from white to brown to black and sometimes have rhizomorphs attached at the bottom. The cap and stem both bruise blue easily when handled.

These psychedelic mushrooms grow from June through to October on disturbed ground in areas with lots of wood debris. They are often found in large groupings.

Psilocybe caerulipes (Blue foot)

Dan Molter/Shroomery.org

Season: May through December

Habitat: Decaying wood, near water systems

Cap: brown, 1-3.5 cm, cone-shaped to convex

Gills: brown to rusty, adnate to sinuate

Stem: 30-60 mm, equal or slightly swollen

Spore print: Dark purple brown

Found across eastern and midwest United States, eastern Canada, and eastern Mexico. This species grows from May through to December, solitarily or in dense clumps on decaying hardwood such as birch, maple, and beech.

The cap ranges from 1-3.5 cm in diameter, is cone-shaped when young, and cinnamon-brown in color. As it ages, it flattens a little bit, becoming more convex in shape, and fades to a light yellow-brown color. When moist, the cap is sticky. The flesh is thin and slowly bruises blue. The gills are light brown when young and become cinnamon-brown with maturity. The stem is 3-6 cm long and whitish when young. As it ages, the stem turns a pallid brown. It is covered with white fibers. When young, the stem is filled with fibers, but it turns hollow with age.

The bluing reaction of this specimen is slow, sometimes taking several hours. It is often found along streams or rivers, after warm rains.

Psilocybe cubensis (Gold caps, Golden tops, Cubes)

Alan Rockefeller/Shroomery.org

Season: May through January

Habitat: Pasture-land on dung

Cap: 1.5-8 cm, cone or bell-shaped, then convex

Gills: gray or dark purple, adnate to adnexed

Stem: 40-150 mm, swollen

Spore print: Dark purple brown

The most well-known hallucinogenic species, P.cubensis is widely distributed as well as being widely cultivated. It grows on cattle dung, and with the expansion of cattle ranching around the world, it has spread widely. It is found in the United States, Mexico, Central America, South America, India, Thailand, and Australia.

This mushroom has a cone-shaped, reddish-brown cap that is between 2-8 cm in diameter. As it matures, the cap flattens out and becomes golden brown in color. When wet, it is sticky. The cap flesh is white and bruises blue when broken and with age. Gills are gray when young, then turn dark purple to black. The stem is 4-15 cm long, hollow, or slightly stuffed, and white or pale yellow in color. It also bruises blue when handled.

P.cubensis contains psilocybin, psilocin, baeocystin, and norbaeocystin. It doesn't just grow on cattle dung but will grow on the dung of other grazing animals like goats and sheep, as well as elephant, yak, ox, and water buffalo. Also, it will grow in fields and gardens spread with manure from these animals. They fruit from May to January in open or tight clumps in meadows and pastures where these animals graze.

Psilocybe cyanescens (Wavy caps, Potent Psilocybe)

CureCat/Shroomery.org

Season: October to February

Habitat: Wood chips, disturbed areas, gardens, mulch

Cap: 2-4 cm, cone-shaped to convex

Gills: cinnamon to dark brown, adnate to subdecurrent

Stem: 20-80 mm, swollen base

Spore print: Dark purple brown

A prolific grower that earns both its' nicknames, P.cyanescens is especially potent and has distinctive wavy caps. There are reports of upwards of 100,000 growing in a single patch! It is a widespread species, found in western and central Europe, western Asia, New Zealand, and the western United States. Its range is continually expanding as it's preferred medium, wood chips and mulch, are also being used more widely. Reports suggest it has successfully colonized many large scale commercial mulch suppliers and thus is making its way around the world.

This mushroom has a smooth chestnut-brown or caramel-colored cap, 1.5-5 cm in diameter, with wavy edges. The cap is convex when young, which flattens out as it matures. When wet, the top is sticky. Gills are light brown when young and become dark purplish brown with maturity. The stem is 3-6 cm long, smooth, and white. Both the cap and stem bruise blue with age and when handled.

P.cyanescens fruits when the temperature drops to 50-65F in autumn and after significant rain, usually between October and February. They grow in large, dense clumps, rarely singularly. These fungi contain psilocybin, psilocin, and baeocystin. Research indicates that North American specimens of this species are some of the most potent of the hallucinogenic mushrooms.

Psilocybe fimetaria

Toxicologia/Shroomery.org

Season: August - November

Habitat: Pastureland, on dung

Cap: 1-3.6 cm, cone-shaped to convex

Gills: clay to dark brown, adnate or sinuate

Stem: 40-65 mm, equal or slightly swollen

Spore print: Dark purple brown

Possibly more widely distributed than currently known, this psychedelic grows on animal dung, in meadows, and in any rich soil. It is known in western United States, Canada, Chile, England, Norway, Finland, and the Czech Republic. It often grows in large rings or groupings, from August to November.

The cap is smooth, light reddish-brown to honey brown, with white flesh that bruises blue when handled. When wet, the cap will peel. Gill are clay-colored when young, then turn dark reddish-brown. The stem is 2-9 cm long, white when young, then turning to yellow or yellow-brown. The stem is covered with white fibers.

Psilocybe hoogshagenii (Los Ninos or Los Chamaquitos ["the little boys"])

Alan Rockefeller/Shroomery.org

Season: June through August

Habitat: coffee plantations

Cap: 1-3 cm, convex, strongly pointed

Gills: coffee color, adnate to adnexed

Stem: 50-90 mm, equal to slightly swollen

Spore print: Dark purple brown

126

This hallucinogenic fungus is found in Mexico, Brazil, Argentina, and Columbia. It fruits in muddy clay soils around coffee plantations in small or large groups or singularly. Enormous flushes that come and go quickly are reported by coffee growers. The season ranges from June to August.

The cap of this mushroom is cone-shaped, smooth, 1-2.5 cm in diameter, and features ridges around it, starting halfway down from the center to the cap. The cone is elongated and pointed, a distinguishable feature, looking like a fairy's hat. It is reddish or orangish-brown and sticky when wet. The gills are brown when young and turn purplish-black with maturity. The stem is hollow, 5-9 cm long, and sometimes twisted. All parts bruise blue when handled.

Psilocybe liniformans (also Psilocybe liniformans var. americana)

Enrique Rubio Domínguez/Asturnatura.com

Season: August through November

Habitat: Pastureland, on horse dung

Cap: 1-2.5 cm, convex

Gills: dark brown, adnexed

Stem: 14-30 mm, equal or slightly swollen

Spore print: Dark grayish purple brown

Growing in pastureland and meadows, this psychedelic is found only in the Netherlands. The American version varies only slightly and is found in Oregon, Washington, and Michigan, as well as Chile.

When young, the cap is reddish-brown. This fades to yellow-brown as it ages. Bell-shaped at first, the cap flattens out with maturity. It is smooth, and when wet, can be peeled. The gills are dark brown. The stem is light yellow and grooved.

The only difference between the Netherlands and American types is that the Netherlands specimen has gills with a gelatinous edge that is easily peeled away. With the American type, the gill edge is not peelable.

Psilocybe pelliculosa

JimmyTheWorm/Shroomery.org

Season: August through October

Habitat: Disturbed woodlands

Cap: .5-2 cm, cone-shaped

Gills: brown, adnate to adnexed

Stem: 60-80 mm, equal to slightly swollen

Spore print: Purplish brown

A species that grows mainly in the Pacific Northwest of the United States, including California, Oregon, Washington, and Idaho, and in British Columbia, Canada. It was once also found in Finland. It is widespread throughout the areas of the Pacific Northwest where it fruits. It grows along logging roads, forest paths, and other disturbed areas. These fungi grow in clusters or groupings on moss and forest debris in areas where firs and alders grow.

The cap is cone-shaped, smooth, and yellow-brown when wet. It becomes pinkish when dry. The cap is easily peeled, especially when wet. When immature, the gills are cinnamon-brown, and they become dark brown with age. The brown stem has a slightly swollen base, and is covered with silky hairs. When handled or bruised, it turns blueish-green.

Psilocybe semilanceata (Liberty cap)

CureCat/Shroomery.org

Season: September through December, sometimes in spring as well

Habitat: Grasslands around dung

Cap: .5-2.5 cm cone-shaped or bell-shaped

Gills: purple-brown, adnexed

Stem: 40-100 mm, equal

Spore print: Dark purple brown

A potent and widespread hallucinogenic, this little mushroom has a distinctive bell-shaped cap with a conical protrusion in the center. It fruits around the world in meadows and pastures that have been fertilized with cow or sheep dung. It does not grow directly on the dung though, instead it lives on the decaying grass roots.

Besides being conical and pointed, the cap is .5-2.5 cm wide and ranges from pale brown to dark brown. The center is generally darker and has a green-blue tinge. As it matures, the cap stays basically the same, though the color will vary depending on the level of hydration. When it is overly dry, it is light brown to yellow-brown. Striations are apparent on the outside of the cap, matching where the gills are on the underside. When wet, the cap is sticky and has a thin gelatinous film that can be peeled back. The gills are light brown when young and become dark gray or brownish purple with age. The stem is 4.5-14 cm long, light yellowish-brown, and often thicker closer to the base. All parts will stain blue when handled.

This species is generally considered to be native to Europe. However, it is now found in at least 35 countries, including most European countries, the United States, Canada, Australia, the Ukraine, and India.

Psilocybe serbica (also known as Psilocybe bohemica)

Kocos/Shroomery.org

Season: Autumn

Habitat: Woodlands, disturbed areas

Cap: 1-5 cm, cone-shaped, then convex

Gills: light or dark brown, adnate to adnexed

Stem: 4.5-10 cm, equal to slightly swollen

Spore print: Purple brown

Fruiting in large groups, this hallucinogenic is found throughout central Europe, and more specifically the Czech Republic, Austria, and Germany. It grows on woody debris around trees, specifically birch, alder, hornbeam, and spruce.

The cap is conical, becoming convex or flat with age. The brown cap is smooth with white flesh that turns blue when bruised. The

132

cap does not peel when wet. Gills are light brown when young, turning dark brown with a purple tinge. The stem is white, with a silky or glossy look, and is slightly swollen at the base. The stem and cap bruise blue when handled.

This mushroom prefers areas around creek beds, roadsides, and forest paths.

Psilocybe strictipes

Season: August - November

Habitat: Grasslands, pasture-land

Cap: .5-3 cm, cone-shaped to convex

Gills: dark brown, adnate or subdecurrent

Stem: 40-70 mm, equal

Spore print: Dark purple brown

This hallucinogenic mushroom is found in Germany, England, France, the Netherlands, Scotland, Slovakia, Siberia, Sweden, Chile, and the Pacific Northwest of the United States. It prefers subarctic locations. It fruits in grassy fields and lawns, often where animals graze but never directly in the dung.

It features a dark rusty-brown cap, 5-30 cm across, usually cone-shaped or convex. As it matures, it flattens and displays a bump in the center of the cap. The surface is smooth, and the top cuticle layer can be peeled off. When young, the gills are cream-colored, they then change to dark purple or brown when mature. The stem is white, 4-10 cm long, and tough. The cap and stem bruise blue when handled.

Psilocybe stuntzii (Blue ringers, Stuntz's blue legs)

Noah Siegel/Shroomery.org

Season: September through December

Habitat: Mulch, gardens, disturbed areas

Cap: 1.5-5 cm, cone-shaped to convex

Gills: brown, adnate to adnexed

Stem: 30-60 mm, equal to slightly swollen

Spore print: Dark purple brown

A hallucinogenic that grows on the west coast of the United States, specifically the Pacific Northwest from July through December. It is not as common as it once was. In places where it does fruit, it is often in massive colonies.

The cap is cone-shaped, 1-2 cm in diameter, smooth, and ranges from dark brown to yellow-brown. As it ages, it becomes paler.

The cap also flattens with age and is generally lighter in the center as compared to the edges. The gills are yellow-brown when young and become purplish-brown with maturity. When young, the stem is stuffed with fibers. It becomes hollow with age. It is 3-6 cm long, sometimes twisted, larger at the base, and ranges from white to light brown in color. All parts of the mushroom stain greenish-blue when handled or injured.

P.stuntzii grows on conifer wood chips, seeming to prefer a species found in the Pacific Northwest. It was found in mulched gardens abundantly for years. Currently, since the conifer populations in this area have been cleared, and therefore not used as often in landscaping, the mushroom is also less common.

Psilocybe subaeruginosa (also known as Psilocybe australiana)

Otto/Shroomery.org

Season: April through August

Habitat: Woodland, disturbed areas, pine plantations, prefers pine (Pinus radiata)

Cap: 1.5-3cm convex to bell-shaped

Gills: cream-colored to violet brown, adnate

Stem: 45-100 mm, equal to slightly swollen

Spore print: Dark purple brown

This species is found in Australia and New Zealand and grows solitarily or in open clusters on mulch, wood chips, and woody forest debris. It fruits from April through to August and is a common species.

The tan cap is 1-6 cm in diameter, and cone-shaped or convex. As it ages, it flattens, though the center and often features a small, pointy bump. The gills are cream-colored when young, then purplish-brown when mature. The stem is white, 4.5-22 cm long, and slightly enlarged near the base. All parts of the mushroom bruise blue when handled. Studies show this species contains psilocybin and little to no psilocin.

Psilocybe subcaerulipes (also known as Psilocybe argentipes)

Alan Rockefeller/Shroomery.org

Season: Unknown

Habitat: Woodland, disturbed landscapes, rich soil with woody debris

Cap: 2.5-6 cm, cone-shaped

Gills: gray to purple, adnate or adnexed

Stem: 60-80 mm, equal or slightly swollen

Spore print: Dark violet brown

A species found only in Asia, specifically Japan, Taiwan, South Korea, and Thailand. It grows in soil that is rich with woody debris and seems to prefer Japanese Blue Oak, Loblolly Pine, and the Sugi tree.

The cap is bell-shaped, chestnut-brown, and 2.5-6 cm in diameter. As it ages, the cap flattens and produces a raised center. When wet, it is darker in color than when dry. Dry, it is a light brown color. The edges of the cap are often wavy. When young, the gills are grayish-orange, then turn to purplish-brown in maturity. The stem is white when young, then it turns yellowish, and finally reddish-brown. It is 6-8 cm long and is wider at the base. It stains blue when handled or bruised.

Research of this mushroom has shown promise for the use of it in the treatment of OCD, based on studies done in mice. In Japanese, it is called Hikageshibiretake, the "shadow numbness mushroom."

Psilocybe yungensis (Genius mushroom)

Alan Rockefeller/Shroomery.org

Season: Summer

Habitat: Rotten wood, coffee plantations

Cap: 1-2.5 cm, cone-shaped

Gills: purple-brown, adnate to adnexed

Stem: 30-50, equal or slightly swollen

Spore print: Dark purple brown

This species fruits in various locations around the world, including northeastern, southeastern, and central Mexico, Ecuador, Colombia, Bolivia, and China. It grows on rotting wood and is often found on coffee plantations and in subtropical areas. It seems to prefer elevations of 1,000-2,000 meters. P.yungensis grows in groups or clusters from June to July, though in Bolivia, it has appeared in January.

It features a bell-shaped reddish-brown to rusty-brown cap, 2-2.5 cm in diameter. When dry, the cap is lighter in color, a yellowish-brown. The cap is smooth, sticky, and features a pronounced bump in the center. The gills are gray when young then become purplish-brown. Hollow and brittle, the stem is between 3-5 cm long. It is pale brown on top, reddish-brown near the bottom, and covered in dense white fibers. The fibers fall off at maturity, leaving a smooth stem. All parts of the mushroom stain blue when handled.

Psilocybe zapotecorum

Alan Rockefeller/Shroomery.org

Season: varies

Habitat: Swampy areas, forests, coffee plantations

Cap: 1-3 cm, cone-shaped or convex or umbonate

Gills: purple brown, sinuate or adnate

Stem: 100-200 mm, equal to slightly swollen

Spore print: Purple-brown

A species found in the subtropical forests of Ecuador, Argentina, Brazil, Chile, Columbia, Peru, Guatemala, Venezuela, and Mexico. Often, it is found in massive clusters, containing upwards of a hundred mushrooms.

The brownish-yellow cap is cone-shaped, with a pointed top, and stays that general shape even in maturity. It usually has a raised center, though sometimes it is depressed. Cap is 2-13 cm in diameter and smooth with a wavy margin. As it matures, the cap color changes to brown and then black. The gills are cream-colored when young and become purplish-brown in maturity. The stem is hollow, 3-26 cm long, and white or gray when young. As it ages, it turns yellowish, then blue, then black. All parts of the mushroom stain blue, then turn black, when handled or injured.

This hallucinogenic grows around creeks, ravines and rivers, preferring humid locations. It is often found in conjunction with oak, pine, magnolia, birch, and ash trees, and around blackberry bushes.

CONCLUSION

Hallucinogenic mushrooms have been used for centuries by indigenous peoples around the world. Their use by each culture is as unique as the species themselves. Research on the exact effects of each species is limited, and mostly incidental. However, there is great promise in their use for achieving altered states and higher consciousness.

Before you consume any mushroom, psychedelic or not, be sure you have identified it 100 percent. The incidents of accidental poisonings are numerous, and quite often occur when one is seeking a hallucinogenic species. A mistake can easily be deadly. Study the mushrooms, seek out experts (not just online!), and don't take chances.

Mushroom foraging is fun, and when you find one of these gems, quite rewarding.

GLOSSARY

Aeruginascin

Closely related to a toxin found on frog skin, aeruginascin is found in two mushroom species, Inocybe aeruginascens, and Pholiotina cyanopus. There are few scientific studies of the effects of aeruginascin on humans. However, it is reported to produce a euphoric effect as opposed to a hallucinogenic one. Aeruginascin is in a category of neurotoxins named indolamines. Melatonin and tryptophan are also indolamine neurotoxins.

Baeocystin

An organic compound found in fungi also containing psilocybin. There isn't much research as to the exact effects of this compound on humans. However, incidental reports state it provides a mild hallucinogenic experience.

DMT (Dimethyltryptamine)

A naturally occurring chemical substance found in a variety of plants and animals. It is consumed as a psychedelic and is touted for its use in spiritual practices. This psychedelic causes alterations in mood, perception, cognition, and consciousness. The quick onset of effects and the relatively short length of mind-alteration are significant keys to its popularity. If inhaled or injected, the effects generally last from five to fifteen minutes. When ingested orally, the effects last three hours or more.

Gymnopilin

A substance found to occur naturally in fungi of the Gymnopilus species. It is a hallucinogenic, although the methods in which it works are still unclear and are being studied.

Norbaeocystin

An organic compound found in mushrooms also containing psilocybin, the exact effects of norbaeocystin on the human body are still being studied. Current studies don't list it as a hallucinogenic on its own. It is believed to assist in synthesizing psilocybin after being consumed, and contribute to the type of high the user experiences.

Psilocin

A close relative of psilocybin, the chemical make-up is slightly different in this naturally occurring substance. However, most psilocybin turns into a type of psilocin in the body after being ingested. The mind-altering effects are comparative to LSD and DMT (Dimethyltryptamine). Effects include euphoria, restlessness, arousal, synesthesia, dilated pupils, and visualization, as well as headaches, chills, sweating, and increased body temperature. Psilocin effects generally last from 1-3 hours. The effects a person will experience are variable and highly subjective.

Psilocybin

A psychedelic that occurs naturally in over 200 mushroom species. It causes mind-altering effects, such as hallucinations, euphoria, distorted sense of time, and changes in perception. It can also cause panic attacks and nausea. The altering effects generally last from two to six hours, although it depends widely on the type of mushroom, the dosage, and the individual consuming it.

Serotonin

A complex naturally-occurring neurotransmitter that is known for its effect of producing feelings of happiness and well-being. It is produced in the human body, in the central nervous system. Serotonin is widespread and found naturally in mammals, insects, plants, and fungi.

Pharmaceutical drugs used to treat depression alter serotonin levels in the user.

Many mushrooms species that contain psilocybin and/or psilocin also contain serotonin.

REFERENCES

Guzmán G. (1983). *The Genus Psilocybe: A Systematic Revision of the Known Species Including the History, Distribution, and Chemistry of the Hallucinogenic Species.*

Guzmán G, Allen JW, Gartz J (2000). "A worldwide geographical distribution of the neurotropic fungi, an analysis and discussion"

Haze, V. & Dr, K. Mandrake, PhD. (2016). *The Psilocybin Mushroom Bible: The Definitive Guide to Growing and Using Magic Mushrooms.* Green Candy Press: Toronto, Canada.

Janikian, M. (2019). *Your Psilocybin Mushroom Companion: An Informative, Easy-to-Use Guide to Understanding Magic Mushrooms—From Tips and Trips to Microdosing and Psychedelic Therapy.* Ulysses Press.

Metzner, R. Ph.D. (2005). *Sacred Mushroom of Visions: Teonanácatl: A Sourcebook on the Psilocybin Mushroom.* Park Street Press.

Miller, R. L., Dr. (2017). *Psychedelic Medicine: The Healing Powers of LSD, MDMA, Psilocybin, and Ayahuasca.* Park Street Press.

Nicholas, L. G. & K. Ogamé (2006). *Psilocybin Mushroom Handbook: Easy Indoor and Outdoor Cultivation.* Quick American Archives.

Oss, O.T. & O.N. Oeric. (1993). *Psilocybin: Magic Mushroom Grower's Guide: A Handbook for Psilocybin Enthusiasts.* (2nd Edition). Quick American Archives.

Powell, S. G. & G. Hancock (2011). *The Psilocybin Solution: The Role of Sacred Mushrooms in the Quest for Meaning.* Park Street Press.

Stamets P. (1996). *Psilocybin Mushrooms of the World: An Identification Guide.* Berkeley, California: Ten Speed Press.

Stamets, P. (2000). *Growing Gourmet and Medicinal Mushrooms.* (3rd Edition). Ten Speed Press.

Printed in Great Britain
by Amazon

12634939R10089